Praise for *My Child's Different*

My Child's Different can provide us all with renewed faith in our own children, regardless of the difficulties we experience with them along the way, and offers plenty of professional advice that will be of benefit to any parent.

**Bonnie Harris, Director, Connective Parenting –
www.connectiveparenting.com – and author of
*When Your Kids Push Your Buttons***

The whole Halligan family should be thanked for their honesty and openness in writing *My Child's Different*, and I think this book will do a great deal of good.

Barry Huggett, OBE, Principal, More House Foundation

Many parents raising a child with SEN can find getting the help they need a struggle, but in *My Child's Different* Elaine Halligan provides hope to these families. Written in an easy-going, down-to-earth tone, this book offers an incredibly insightful and honest account of her own family's journey and provides useful strategies that parents can use with their children.

**Naomi Richards, life coach, The Kids Coach –
www.thekidscoach.org.uk – and author of
The Parent's Toolkit and *Being Me (and Loving It)***

My Child's Different is a wonderful guide to navigating the choppy waters of parenthood. With wit, warmth and wisdom, Elaine Halligan shows us how to help our children overcome the toughest obstacles to find their own place in the world.

Carl Honoré, author of *In Praise of Slow* and *Under Pressure*

In *My Child's Different* Elaine Halligan has had the imagination and the wisdom to tell her story both as a mother and as someone with skills and training in parenting education. It is a mother's story told from the heart that many will identify with, and indeed learn many pearls of wisdom from.

**Judy Reith, parenting coach, author
Parenting Pe**

D0315544

A must-read for any parent bringing up a child who is seen as 'different' or 'difficult'. The unique combination of her personal account of Sam's troubled early years together with the contributions of positive parenting expert Melissa Hood makes this a practical, inspirational read for any parent worried about what the future looks like for their child.

Susan Stiffelman, marriage and family therapist and author of *Parenting without Power Struggles* and *Parenting with Presence*

Elaine and Sam's journey is an incredible story of hope, and its retelling in this book is perfectly balanced with positive parenting theory, practical guidance and the intense unconditional love that all parents will relate to. Every parent needs to read *My Child's Different*.

Paul Dix, Executive Director, Pivotal Education and author of *When the Adults Change, Everything Changes*

An important book that will undoubtedly change many lives for the better, *My Child's Different* is also a must-read for educators and anyone working with children so that they can gain a better understanding of how to support their challenging students, and be able to recommend this book to their families.

Kelly Pietrangeli, author and 'Mama Motivator', Project Me for Busy Mothers

I love this book! Beautifully written with marvellous clarity and candour, Elaine Halligan's narrative shares the ups and downs, the daily challenges, the small sequential steps forward and the heartbreaks and triumphs of parenting Sam.

Sam's story is one of remarkable ultimate success, but the book is not a sugarcoated 'Pollyanna' account – rather it is one filled with exquisite details of the two-steps-forward-one-step-back experience of raising a child with a significant disability. Further gifts for the reader include insights from Sam's therapist, and even commentary from Sam himself.

Emily Perl Kingsley, former director, National Down Syndrome Congress and former writer, *Sesame Street*

My Child's DIFFERENT

The lessons learned from one family's
struggle to unlock their son's potential

Elaine Halligan

with contributions from Melissa Hood

Crown House Publishing Limited
www.crownhouse.co.uk

First published by

Crown House Publishing
Crown Buildings, Bancyfelin, Carmarthen, Wales, SA33 5ND, UK
www.crownhouse.co.uk

and

Crown House Publishing Company LLC
PO Box 2223, Williston, VT 05495, USA
www.crownhousepublishing.com

© Elaine Halligan, 2018

Pages 4–5, 12–16, 29–34, 55–60, 81–85, 103–107, 122–126,
140–144, 157–161 contributions © Melissa Hood.

The right of Elaine Halligan to be identified as the author of this
work has been asserted by her in accordance with the Copyright,
Designs and Patents Act 1988.

First published 2018. Reprinted 2018, 2019 (twice).

All rights reserved. Except as permitted under current legislation no part of this work
may be photocopied, stored in a retrieval system, published, performed in public,
adapted, broadcast, transmitted, recorded or reproduced in any form or by any means,
without the prior permission of the copyright owners. Enquiries should be addressed to
Crown House Publishing.

Pages 28–29 Welcome to Holland © Emily Perl Kingsley. Reproduced with kind permission.

Crown House Publishing has no responsibility for the persistence or accuracy of URLs for
external or third-party websites referred to in this publication, and does not guarantee that any
content on such websites is, or will remain, accurate or appropriate.

British Library of Cataloguing-in-Publication Data

A catalogue entry for this book is
available from the British Library.

Print ISBN 978-178583328-1
Mobi ISBN 978-178583343-4
ePub ISBN 978-178583344-1
ePDF ISBN 978-178583345-8

LCCN 2018936684

Printed and bound in the UK by
Gomer Press, Llandysul, Ceredigion

Disclaimer

While all the stories in this book are true, some names have been
changed to protect the privacy of those involved.

Foreword

'Does positive parenting work with a challenging child?'

This is the most common question I hear from parents when I describe my approach to parenting. Positive parenting is simply parenting that focuses on a loving connection with the child rather than using control techniques like punishment and shame, so logically it should 'work' with any human. But with challenging children, parents are often desperate. They see that their child is 'out of control' and they can't imagine that there's a compassionate way to get their child back on track.

The book you are holding – *My Child's Different* – is the answer to this question. Elaine Halligan's true story of her family's journey with a child who is different (her son Sam) engages the reader from the start. Her heartfelt account describes many incidents of anguish and embarrassment on the journey to gradual discovery and growth, and allows the reader to experience travelling the very potholed road that is living with a child of difference.

As this story unfolds, you see the transformation of an angry, struggling child into a capable, reflective, wonderful young man. What makes that transformation possible is the transformation of his parents, who learn the positive parenting approach that brings out the best in their son.

But this story is not just Elaine's (or even Sam's). This story has the ability to shape the lives of other families, maybe yours.

If you have a differently wired child, you know it. You also know that your child doesn't necessarily respond as other children do to the 'strategies' suggested by all those well-meaning people who insist on giving you advice on raising a child. Maybe you sometimes wonder how you can get through to a child who at times seems impossible to reach.

You may have a child who has a sensory processing issue, an attention deficit of some kind, or severe anxiety that leads to rages. Your child may be very bright but underperforming at school or not connecting so well with their peers. Your child may be the one who is *always* in trouble at school. Maybe they're highly impulsive, have trouble managing their emotions and lash out, beyond the age when other kids seem to be able to control their feelings. Maybe they've been diagnosed with dyslexia, high functioning autism or oppositional defiant disorder. Or your child may not have been labelled with any of the usual acronyms, but their temperament is so intense or sensitive as to set them apart from other, 'easier' kids.

Children like this get used to constant negative feedback, correction and criticism. It's not their parents' fault – these kids are a handful and just getting through the day with them would wear out any parent. But by the time these kids get to school, their self-esteem is already eroded. Then, when they try to cope in school and find it hard – to focus, to learn, to manage their bodies and emotions – their frustration and anxiety explodes.

Is there a way to respond to the behaviour of a child like this that helps them manage their anxiety and anger, that motivates them to persevere when learning is tough, that supports them to become their best selves? We know that the conventional parenting approach of reprimands, nagging, lectures, threats and punishment just makes things worse. In this book, Elaine Halligan describes another way: the positive parenting skills that turned things around with her son.

As Elaine and her husband Tony learned to use descriptive praise, Sam's sense of self-worth started to improve, and as he felt more successful, he became more cooperative. When they began to validate Sam's feelings of anger, hopelessness and frustration, he felt more connected to his parents and more motivated to follow their rules – and he gained the capacity to manage his emotions more effectively. As they learned to respond constructively to unwanted behaviours without making Sam feel worse or damaging his self-esteem, he began to take responsibility and learn from his mistakes.

And so Sam blossomed into a confident young man who became a leader at school and an entrepreneur in life.

Elaine's personal story is told through the lens of her work as a parenting coach, which enriches her perspective and the lessons for readers. Her business partner of nine years at The Parent Practice, Melissa Hood, was Elaine's guide throughout much of her odyssey with Sam – and she adds to the value of *My Child's Different* by contributing her own perspective to each chapter, analysing what was happening with Sam at each stage and giving practical advice on how parents can support their children to be their best.

If you have a child who is different in any way, you'll identify with much of Elaine's experience. You'll smile ruefully at the story of Sam's animal escapades and cringe in sympathy over his science lab tribulations. The Halligans' battles with the authorities in getting the support Sam needed and their navigation of the complex education and health systems may resonate with you. But above all, this book will offer hope to any parent.

My Child's Different is an inspiring success story, and not just because Sam, at 22, is showing every sign of realising his full potential. This is a story of what can be overcome when parents really believe in their child – and of what makes the difference.

Dr Laura Markham

Acknowledgements

I have a list of fifty things to do before I die, and I have to confess that writing a book has never featured on that list! However, as friends and family watched Sam's life unfold, I have lost count of the number of times they encouraged me to put pen to paper and tell his story. I also felt I had to wait till he was of an age where he could agree, or not, to his story being told. This book is the culmination of years of positive parenting, and Sam is fully on board with sharing his experiences.

Thank you, first, to my incredible family. To Tony, my wonderful husband, who has been my rock throughout our three decades together, coping through thick and thin and helping me keep my sanity. His selflessness continues to be a theme throughout our marriage. He is a giver and an incredibly generous person. If it had not been for you arriving in South Africa as a homeless Kiwi, we would never have met! And to my fabulously independent and amazing daughter Izzy, who has endured much, and shows great maturity. I sometimes wonder who is parenting whom, as she has an emotional intelligence beyond her years.

To Mum and Dad, who are the most supportive, positive and encouraging parents a daughter could wish for.

To my remarkable business partner Melissa Hood, who taught me all I needed to know about positive parenting and who has been there over the years to help us through each emotional crisis. Her authoritative voice provides the parental guidance in this book. Without her constant support, wisdom and compassion, I am certain I would not have been in a position to write it at all.

To my book mastermind/coach, Alison Jones, for her unfailing belief that I could accomplish this, and for guiding me step by step in pulling the story together. All that time spent together, interviewing Sam as a young adult, and transcribing his innermost thoughts and feelings, was a powerful, cathartic process and one, I realised with hindsight, that needed to be done.

To my truly gifted and talented editor, Julia Slone-Murphy, who was able to tap into my mindset and work her magic with my words to bring the story to life.

To Annabel, our Australian au pair, who was a breath of fresh air for us all and whose colourful personality, energy and passion ensured the children were well cared for. Her perceptiveness and insight were remarkable for someone so young. Now with three children herself, she is a warm and empathetic mum.

To the gorgeous Hayley, our South African au pair, who is now married to a Zambian farmer. Together, they run a chicken business and have their own clutch of children. She has also set up a local school. She credits her adept parenting skills to the experience she had with us. I say it was a baptism of fire for her at such a young age, but it certainly played a part in making her the very resourceful and solution-focused young woman she is today.

To all Sam's teachers over the years. The positive influence good teachers can have on a child's life is incredible, and, to my eyes, the teaching profession is one of the most noble in the world. We entrust teachers with our children, not only to educate them but also to nurture their minds, and I believe they matter more to a student's achievement than any other aspect of schooling. For Sam, the teachers at Knowl Hill School, in particular, listened carefully to his needs and differentiated their routine to enable him to cope. I will forever be grateful for that.

Thank you to Mrs Stiff, Sam's form tutor at More House School. Patience should be her middle name, and her kindness and compassion ensured Sam's success in his first year.

To Mr Morgan, who not only taught Sam product design (the revolving coffee table Sam made in his class, with hidden storage and lifting table top, is still in good use today) but also showed him true grit and resourcefulness.

To Mr James Babbage, the new business studies teacher with just one A level student: Sam. They made a formidable team, with James teaching Sam business studies, and Sam trying to teach James golf. They still spend many a weekend on the golf course together. ('You just need to invest some time in getting a good golf coach to teach you the basics,' Sam loves to say. 'A good teacher can make all the difference, James!')

To Mrs Rouse, for inspiring Sam in art and pottery and for allowing his creativity to flourish.

To Mr Kirkham, who, as head of sixth form, encouraged Sam to apply for the role of head boy and allowed him to develop his leadership style unconstrained.

To all my clients who are parents and to my friends, who read the sample chapters and gave me such encouraging feedback. I so appreciate your time and valuable, insightful comments. You know who you are and there are so many of you to thank. It was your feedback and encouragement that helped shape this dream into a reality.

I also thank you, dear reader, for choosing this book. It is a testament to your commitment to your family, and shows that you are curious and willing to learn. I hope this book can support you in taking the next steps to unlocking your child's potential.

And finally, the greatest thanks go to our son, Sam. A natural entrepreneur, Sam really does add value to people's lives, in terms of contributing to their happiness and enjoyment of life. Throughout his education, teachers liked him and helped him. What's fascinating is that he has no comprehension of why they did so. He doesn't know what they saw in him, yet the qualities he possesses are so clear to everyone else: he has an infectiously positive outlook on life, an ability to make people feel good about themselves, a creative mind, an ability to problem-solve, and a great sense of humour, not to mention an incredible spirit for adventure that is anxiety inducing for this mum! At last, that brilliant diamond I always sensed was there is now gleaming for all to see.

Contents

Contents

Introduction

Love recognizes no barriers. It jumps hurdles, leaps fences, penetrates walls to arrive at its destination full of hope.

Attributed to Maya Angelou, American poet, memoirist and civil rights activist

For the past fourteen years, my family and I have been riding a rollercoaster. Not the fast, fun, three-minute ride you can walk away from afterwards, but the emotional kind. You know the one. The kind that rattles you around and strips you raw, that elates you and thrills you, overwhelms and terrifies you. It's exhilarating and exhausting and lasts a lifetime and yet somehow, looking back, might feel like a moment. We have lived it all: from utter despair and hopelessness to profound joy and the greatest celebrations of life.

This book is about our son, Sam.

By the time he was seven, Sam had been excluded from three schools and was burdened with a plethora of diagnostic abbreviations that led to him becoming known as the Alphabet Kid. He was incredibly impulsive and had little self-control. As a family, we spent many years in crisis. Sam began to feel very different and inadequate, and we began to think his future was in a young offenders' institution. We knew he was a good and capable boy with a strong moral compass, but it took us many years to really understand his needs and temperament and to realise that his difficulties were varied and complex.

Society expects children, and adults, to conform. We are quick to judge those who present differently, and if our children behave inappropriately we often believe this behaviour is a reflection on our parenting, and that any criticism is directed at us.

The notion that our children may be shunned by society for being different breaks our hearts, and being judged by others can be one of a parent's biggest fears. It is something I experienced regularly.

One of my friends, who has a teenage son on the autistic spectrum, describes the situation with clarity: 'By far the hardest part is the exclusion that families like ours suffer. You see it in the eyes of people you've just met when they can't wait to get away from your child. It's very painful.'

We never gave up on Sam. Over the years, we tried almost every behavioural, physical, emotional and pharmaceutical treatment and programme available. I have put it all in this book – from the bewildering array of Sam's assessments and diagnoses, on-the-floor public tantrums and struggles in unsuitable mainstream education, to fleeting glimpses of hope, significant breakthroughs and, ultimately, achievements we never could have imagined in those early years.

I often tell people that our young Sam was like a stone covered in mud. Over time, as we gained new skills and better resources, we were able to work at this stone, carefully whittling down through his difficulties, fears and stresses, until we had lifted every layer that had been obscuring him and there discovered a brilliant, sparkling diamond – a young man who has kindness, resilience and clarity of vision, as well as an inner strength and confidence that belie his past experiences.

A transformative figure in this story is Melissa Hood. Founder of The Parent Practice, she was our parenting coach, our salvation, and is now one of our dearest friends. If she hadn't come into our lives when she did, I am not sure what would have happened to us all as a family unit. Our journey led me to parenting coaching too, and Melissa and I are now partners at The Parent Practice.

I've gone from feeling an overriding sense of failure in my abilities as a mother to believing that, as parents, the biggest impact we have on our children's lives is through the power of our words.

This is the story of how the 'different', 'difficult' boy became a capable, confident young man, and what we discovered on the journey. Our intention is to inspire and encourage you on your own journey, and maybe help you find the strategies that will make that journey a better experience, with a better outcome, for everyone involved.

You, too, can learn to unlock your child's potential

My wish is that this book conveys hope.

You may be a parent, a grandparent, a bonus parent in a blended family, a teacher, a learning support assistant or a therapist – whatever your role, you want to help a child and maximise their potential.

Perhaps, like Sam, your child is different in some way. Perhaps they've been diagnosed with specific learning needs, or you just sense something isn't quite right. Perhaps you find your child tricky to handle, but don't know what the problem is or how to fix it. Or you may simply have an overwhelming sense that, for a variety of reasons, socially or intellectually, your child is often misunderstood.

You are the expert on your child. And while you may be feeling overwhelmed or anxious about the future, if you are reading this book, you have not given up on your child or on finding ways to move beyond where you are now.

You are the biggest influence on your child's mindset. The power of your words and actions can have a massive impact on their self-worth.

This book is a chronological story of Sam's formative years, from birth to young adulthood. In each chapter, you will glean insight into how Sam felt and what his thoughts and beliefs were at each stage of his schooling. You will also hear Melissa's professional insight and pragmatic parenting advice that you, too, can use. We all want to ensure our children are happy and successful and that they enter adulthood with high self-esteem and sufficient resilience to cope with whatever life throws at them. Melissa will show you how to get into action quickly in your own families, with your own 'different' or 'difficult' children.

Sam has had an incredible impact not only on our lives as a family but also on others around him. His development has been wonderful to watch and be involved in, and I hope by sharing my personal – as well as professional – experience, this book will give you hope, optimism and guidance.

All the best in raising your children. You are their rock, you are their inspiration, and you are never going to give up!

Melissa says: My first meeting with the Halligans

I first met the Halligans when they came to the behavioural centre where I worked. Sam was seven. At some point during our meeting, he got upset and brought his fist down with his entire weight behind it onto his mother's already sore foot, causing her a great deal of pain. He was a very angry little boy.

And with good reason. There's always a reason. You'll read here about his history and understand why he had so much stored frustration, and you'll begin to see why he could not express it any other way.

One of the things I noticed about Sam during our first meetings was his acute powers of observation. I praised him for his perceptiveness and talked about how paying attention to detail was such a useful quality. He immediately responded with a big grin. This very impulsive boy had never seen himself as someone who could slow down enough to notice things that others didn't. I thought, 'We can work with this boy'!

I've now known Elaine and Tony for fourteen years. Never before had I witnessed such dedication in two parents to making life good for their children in the face of overwhelming difficulties. The Halligans completely embraced the positive parenting skills I taught them and found support for Sam through different therapies and educational provision.

What he has achieved could not have been predicted when he was seven, and his parents' belief in him played no small part in his growth in self-worth.

1

Us, and Our
Blue-Eyed Boy

(The Calm Before the Storm)

*The greatest gift a couple can give their baby is a loving relationship,
because that relationship nourishes Baby's development.*

John M. Gottman and Julie Schwartz Gottman,
And Baby Makes Three

I come from a loving, caring family that does not judge. The
values of giving and putting others first were instilled in me
from an early age by both my parents.

My memories of being a tween are of helping my mother
run the shop at the local mental health hospital on the out-
skirts of Edinburgh. I loved playing shopkeeper, taking money
and selling over the counter, although I realise now that the
experiences I had there were more profound than I appreciated at the time. At this young age, I was interacting with
adults with severe mental health disorders, and it was an
important introduction for me to people with differences.
Now in her late seventies, my mother still devotes herself to
serving others: helping at the local hospice four days a week,
which she says feels like a full-time job, and preparing teas at
her local cricket club.

My father is a born optimist, a sensitive and kindly man
who inspires people around him. He has never been afraid to
show emotion and is always one of the first to well up when
he talks about how proud he is of his grandchildren. He con-
nects well with people and always treats others with respect
and kindness, making time to talk to everyone, from the corner shop owner to the bin-collection people. The two phrases

(and the values they reflect) I attribute to him are: 'When speaking to people, be interested and interesting' and 'You create your own luck'.

Being brought up on these notions of kindness, openness, curiosity and tenacity enabled me to engage others in conversation and resulted in many serendipitous encounters with people who remain significant in my life today. It also gave me the mindset to grasp opportunities, keep exploring possibilities, give things a go and not be fearful of failing.

Without these attributes and the support and empathy of my parents, I really don't know how I would have survived the challenges I faced with Sam. Their nurturing and positive teachings ensured I had the mindset, resilience and determination to never give up on him.

As a young adult, I graduated from the University of Edinburgh with a degree in law and a thirst for adventure. My family, friends and tutors all expected me to practice in Scotland. Instead, I headed to South Africa.

The year was 1988 and everyone in the UK was petitioning against apartheid and marching to free Nelson Mandela. It was the decade when supermarkets all over the country were refusing to buy South African produce and corporations were boycotted for their involvement in the apartheid government. *Cry Freedom* had just been released, but the police seized copies of the film following bombings at screenings, saying it threatened public safety. It was just about the most risky thing to do to go and visit South Africa at that time, but an opportunity presented itself and, despite opposition from family and friends, I grabbed it. I had one year to pursue my dream of seeing more of the world.

It turned out to be one of the best decisions of my life as it was there that, at twenty-two years of age, I met the most wonderful, laid-back, cool and caring Kiwi – Tony.

Life was pretty idyllic. During the week we worked hard in Johannesburg, but the weekends would bring unforgettable spontaneous adventures and escapades, from partying day and night at luxury hotels and casinos in Sun City, light years away from apartheid South Africa, to exploring the Wild Coast with its stunning, rugged, unspoiled coastline and footprint-free beaches. It was the home of the Xhosa tribes and it was like being in a time warp, so tranquil and so far removed from the frenzy of modern city life. Thirsty for more, we travelled across Malawi, Zambia and Zimbabwe. We fell in love with Africa, and with each other. When our year was up, we decided to stay together. I returned to Edinburgh, and Tony came to London. Life was golden and full of promise. We were young and passionate and ready for our next adventure and …

We became accountants. It wasn't the inspiring life I'd imagined, faced with the prospect of studying for account-ancy exams, my man hundreds of miles away, with the London–Edinburgh railway feeling like a second residence, but we were both satisfied with the good careers ahead of us, and our lives were comfortable.

Two years later, Tony's work permit expired. The only way he could remain in the UK was by having a British wife! We faced a significant decision. We wanted to be together, but we were also determined not to be forced by circumstance into a marriage of convenience. So instead, as cinema audi-ences around the world were enjoying *Green Card*, we were living the very process the film portrays. We built a case with reams of evidence supporting the existence of our relation-ship. I managed to obtain special dispensation to miss one of my exams (a privilege reserved for life-or-death situations), and after in-depth interviews at the Home Office in London, we were finally declared common-law husband and wife. Spouses, but not married; committed, but independent. With this arrangement, Tony was granted leave to remain, and our future together was secured.

I called Mum and Dad back in Edinburgh and told them the news. Mum, having not fully understood the logistics of the process, nearly fainted at the other end of the line, exclaiming, 'But where was the wedding, darling?'

Eventually, when the time was right, I moved to London to be with Tony and, out of love and mutual commitment, not convenience, we decided to marry for real. The next step in the journey was to start our family. Although we had talked about having children, the extent of our musings was 'How many shall we have?', 'Private or state education?', and 'I'm quite fond of the name Sam.'

Day one

One of the biggest failings in our society is the silence that mothers keep about what mums-to-be should expect of childbirth.

It is a truly miraculous event. It can empower you with vitality and a sense of pride beyond anything you've ever experienced before, leaving you feeling like an Earth Mother, a natural goddess, at peace and glowing with a formidable love.

But no one tells you the real facts or the gory details. That when your waters break, this doesn't necessarily mean the baby is coming *right now*. That as you're pushing for the baby, you might poo yourself instead. And that when you are only two centimetres dilated after twenty-four hours of labour, there's still a long, long way to go.

I was twenty-nine years old when I gave birth to Sam. He was due on 19 December 1995, so my father, who was born on Christmas Day, was beside himself with excitement at the thought he may share his birthday with another family member. Sam, however, had other plans; he was very comfortable indeed. My parents came down from Scotland to help with the arrival but, after ten days of waiting, had to go back home. I was eventually booked into hospital on New Year's Eve to be induced. Tony and I celebrated a very quiet

Hogmanay in the maternity ward as I was very uncomfortable. Then it began.

The birth was traumatic. I have a vivid recollection of screaming for pain relief, only to find the nurses attending to my husband, as he'd fainted from the sight of all the blood across the sheets. At one point the obstetrician had to wipe her glasses. A ventouse delivery was attempted and failed, and I came close to having a blood transfusion. Finally, they brought out the forceps.

At 6 a.m. on 2 January 1996, after thirty-two hours of labour, Sam was born.

Weighing in at a hefty ten pounds (4.5 kg), he looked as if he had just completed a bout with Mike Tyson in the boxing ring, badly marked on his face and bruised all over. But to me, he was a piece of heaven. I felt complete. I had my beautiful, blonde, blue-eyed boy and I fell head-over-heels in love. I was tired but ever so happy. The birth had been a challenge and Sam was covered in meconium, but the nurses wiped him down, stitched me up and assured me that everything was fine, and I got on with my new task of being a mum.

Six months later, I had a strange appointment at the hospital. I was asked to meet with the senior registrar, who wanted to know if Sam was OK and informed me that, by the way, my hospital notes had disappeared. Even at that point, I didn't stop to question whether my birth had been normal. I was so naïve. I reported back that everything was rosy, and I was sure the notes would turn up someday soon.

Little Buddha

Sam was the perfect 'Buddha baby'. He did lots of observing and listening, sitting and smiling, and was calm and happy. He slept well, ate well and, while others around him were crawling around and getting up to mischief, Sam was at his happiest when he had food or a bottle of milk close to hand. Mealtimes were easy; he would open his mouth like a bird to get fed. After about three months, Tony and I started to socialise again, feeling content and relaxed leaving Sam with a babysitter, knowing he was in a good sleep-time routine and would rarely wake up once put down. My other new-mum friends were complaining of their babies' teething and colic and feeding issues, devouring books about parenting, delving into the secrets of the 'contented little baby' and swotting up on child development with Dr Spock. But I was the 'blissfully contented parent' they strived to be. What could a book tell me that I didn't instinctively know? I had everything in hand, and loved being a mum. Parenting didn't seem that hard to me. I was convinced that all that our children need is love and nurturing.

Melissa says: The importance of preparing for parenthood

Elaine and Tony were not alone in entrusting their early parenting to instinct. Today, in the internet age, new parents often do a lot of online research about the practical aspects of caring for a baby and the early developmental milestones. In that sense, my own son and his wife were vastly better prepared for the birth of their first child than I had been for the birth of mine.

But most parents-to-be, even today, don't really discuss how they want to raise a child and what their aspirations are for this new person. Much is assumed. And no amount of reading can really prepare you for the impact becoming a family has on your relationship and lifestyle.

Most new parents experience a change in relationships both with their partner and with others. Research from the Gottman Institute shows that almost 70 per cent of men and women experience a decline in relationship satisfaction after the first baby is born, with reduced sleep and intimacy, changes in roles and, for some, postnatal depression. But the birth of a baby can also create a very strong bond between the parents as they take on new responsibility for another life. They often feel united by their shared love for the new baby. A couple may act more as a team than ever before. Having a baby can help a couple become more flexible and creative. Becoming a parent provides an opportunity to reassess values and goals. Grown-ups can get in touch with their fun, playful side. Babies and young children can teach adults to wonder and marvel at simple things and experience the joy of discovery. Children are great teachers – we learn a lot about ourselves through our interactions with them.

Elaine and Tony certainly learned a lot from Sam.

So often we prepare for birth by attending classes, reading books, designing a nursery, buying (a huge amount of) equipment, creating a birth plan and packing a hospital bag well in advance. But, as with Sam's birth, plans often fly out the window. Babies don't read the plans! But even if the birthing process is straightforward, that's where the plans cease for many of us. What about the next eighteen, twenty-one, fifty-plus years?

Many of us think parenting is supposed to be instinctive, especially if we had happy childhoods. We think we'll just do it like Mum and Dad did (or we may plan to do it differently, but find ourselves defaulting to their parenting model anyway). But our children are not the same as we were, and we are not our parents. And we are not parenting in the same circumstances. What we think are instincts are really deeply ingrained habits or attitudes that may not be best suited to this child. We need to be well-informed first before we can rely on our instincts. And we should not be afraid to ask for support, as this is the most difficult job we'll ever do.

If you haven't yet started a family but plan to, then it's a really good idea to talk to your partner now about how you want to raise your children. You may not really know what you think until you start to talk about it. My husband and I have our best conversations while we're walking our dogs. There's something about the fact that we're moving that gets the creative juices going. But you can also have a great 'family planning' conversation over a meal or on a car journey. And you'll probably need more than one conversation. Just make sure you're face to face or you'll miss out on 80 per cent of the communication, which is non-verbal.

Even if you've already got children it's worth having a version of this conversation.

Discuss your own childhoods, what you loved about them and would want to replicate, and what you would do differently. Each parent comes from a different family culture even if you come from the same place and share the same ethnicity. Your habits, practices, rituals, beliefs and values will be different in small or large ways. Some of these may not really show up until you have a child in front of you and are dealing with a situation where you both have quite different views. But try to anticipate as much as you can by discussing some of these points:

- How big a family do you want?

- Do either of you feel as if you might have more of an affinity for boys or girls? Why?

- Do you want your extended families to be involved in your children's lives? How much? In what way? (Contributing factors will of course include distance and how close each parent is with their family.)

- Can you each identify your style of communication? Is it words or actions? Do you blow up quickly but subside equally fast or are you likely to seethe with resentment for a long time? Does this come from your family of origin? Were there any taboo topics in your family?

- Did you talk about emotions in your family?

- What was the style of discipline?

- How was conflict resolved?

- Is some kind of faith experience or spirituality important to you?

- What are your thoughts around education? Private or state school? Single-sex or co-ed? Highly academic or a more rounded approach?

- Is it important to you that your children be active/play sports?

- Are you musical? Would you want your child to know music in some way?

- Are family holidays important to you? Would you want to reproduce the holidays of your childhood or not?

- What memories would you like to lay down with your children?

- How aware are you of your own temperament? Is that different from your partner's?

- What strengths do/will you bring to parenthood? What characteristics do you feel you will you need to modify?

- What attitudes, characteristics or values would you like to encourage in your children? For example, integrity, respect, work ethic, confidence.

There will be many other questions that will pop up as you chat.

Dr John Gottman suggests that when parents discuss their values they try to work out which aspects are non-negotiable and which parts they're prepared to compromise on. When I did his couples counselling course he used as an example two competing values held by each parent; education and spending time together as a family. The example he gave was about saving for the children's future education vs spending money on a family holiday now. Other conflicts might include a debate over the merits of boarding school as the best form of education vs having the child living at home. Or spending a lot of time in enriching after-school activities vs chilling out with the family.

Whenever conflict arises in the day-to-day hurly-burly of family life, it is important that the couple – who are the bedrock of the family unit and the child's model of how to handle conflict – manage disputes in ways that respect each of them.

Here are some healthy ways to deal with conflict:

- Acknowledge, validate and reflect back your partner's point of view to him/her, especially where this is different from yours.

- When there is conflict between you, don't criticise, but make requests and state your needs – e.g. 'I need more help around the house. Please can you take out the bins each week.'

- State how you feel using 'I' statements, not 'you' statements – e.g. 'When you leave the kitchen in a mess I feel as if you expect me to clean it up and I feel taken for granted.' not 'You always leave the kitchen untidy – you really take me for granted.'

- Confine yourself to the matter under discussion – don't bring up history. Don't use the words 'always' or 'never'.

- Avoid defensiveness. This means denying any responsibility for a problem – e.g. Maggie has a sharp intake of breath after Steve just braked hard in the car and he says: 'There you go again being a back-seat driver!' Or Raoul, in response to his partner's complaints about the state of the kitchen: 'I'm not messy – you have OCD – nobody can live like this!' Accept some personal responsibility for at least part of the problem. 'Sorry! That was a bit abrupt.' 'I guess my cleaning standards aren't quite the same as yours, are they?' It's easier to accept responsibility if your partner usually appreciates you.

- Avoid stonewalling. This means the listener withdraws from the interaction and doesn't respond. It indicates an emotional withdrawal from the relationship. If you feel overwhelmed and need to withdraw, ask for a break and agree upon a time to resume the conversation.

When you've had an argument, make repairs – e.g. say sorry or use humour or try to see your partner's point of view; anything that stops negativity escalating.

Your relationship is the blueprint for your child's future relationships. So while it's not bad for children to see their parents argue, make sure they see how you resolve things too.

Elaine and Tony were in the calm before the storm and Elaine found the early days fairly easy as the 'blissfully contented parent'. But this is not the same for all parents. For Elaine and Tony the larger debates and topics for discussion were yet to come, as the storm clouds were brewing.

Elaine's reflections

1. Preparing for parenthood is a huge change in any couple's relationship and lifestyle. Hindsight showed us we were poorly prepared and had not spent time discussing our key values in bringing up our baby. What steps will you take to set up for success and agree some shared values?

2. There is a plethora of parenting books parents can read to arm themselves with knowledge. How are you preparing for your new arrival?

3. For many, parenting is not instinctive, but rather results from a deeply conditioned state that depends on the parent's own experiences and upbringing. Have you made a conscious decision to parent differently from, or to follow in the footsteps of, your own parents and their values?

Further reading

John M. Gottman and Julie Schwartz Gottman, *And Baby Makes Three: The Six-Step Plan for Preserving Marital Intimacy and Rekindling Romance After Baby Arrives*, 2008.

2

I'm Sure It'll All Be Fine

(Pre-School)

When processing is disorderly, the brain cannot do its most important job of organizing sensory messages.

Carol Stock Kranowitz, *The Out-of-Sync Child*

We holidayed that first autumn in Portugal and it was a breeze. So the following year we decided to travel to New Zealand and introduce Sam to the Kiwi 'rellies'.

I'll never forget that flight to Christchurch.

Sam had just started to walk. Imagine: thirty-two hours door-to-door (with a stopover in Singapore), and your son suddenly discovers a new mobility – and boy, does he want to practise! Tony and I spent much of the flight trying to contain him.

There were none of the luxuries of personalised in-flight entertainment we enjoy today. This was 1997 and there was one large video screen for all to view. Sam, a rather large baby, would sleep for a few hours, then suddenly sit up in his bassinet, blocking the whole video screen for the rest of the passengers behind us. They were not happy, and understandably so. You may have already experienced a long-haul flight with children, or perhaps you're planning one. If we knew then what we know now, I'm sure we would have tried to find the money for a proper seat for Sam.

Next, Sam felt it was time to get moving, so off he wobbled. He hadn't got far before he let out an earth-shattering scream. We found him standing motionless in front of a Sikh gentleman who was wearing a bright yellow turban. The man was smiling blankly at Sam, while Sam was screaming back at him as if his life depended on it. Gathering Sam up into my arms, I apologised profusely to the gentleman. 'I'm so sorry, I think my son must have got a fright when he spotted your turban. He's never seen one up close before. I'm sorry if we caused you any embarrassment.' Thankfully, he took it in good humour. Walking back to our seat, wishing the ground would swallow me up, I consoled myself with the thought that the situation wasn't dissimilar to a young child seeing Father Christmas for the first time; that jolly old man with rosy cheeks, a big tummy, and a long beard can be, quite frankly, terrifying!

My mother and father – now Granny Mavis and Grandpa John – counselled me wisely from the day Sam was born. 'You need to look after yourself,' they would say. 'And your relationship. Work hard to stop yourself becoming a unit dedicated purely to Sam.' They felt so strongly about this that they made an agreement that Tony and I were to have a weekend away and a whole week off from our parental duties every year and they would come to London from Edinburgh to take care of Sam. I didn't realise at the time how lucky we were to have such a supportive and energetic set of grandparents who adored their grandson. (In time, I began to appreciate that this generosity was not something experienced by many of my friends.)

At playgroups, the other children would love getting stuck in to messy play with sand and mud and finger paints, but Sam would avoid these activities and wander off to do something else. If he did get in the sandpit, it would be to throw sand at another child or snatch their bucket from them.

He hated having different foods together on his plate and would complain vociferously when foods touched. Chips and ketchup couldn't be too close. Potatoes and peas were to be kept apart (no mean feat, with the peas rolling around on the dish).

Hair washing and nail cutting became stressful experiences, and with the screams he emitted at bath time our neighbours would be forgiven for thinking we were sticking hot needles in his eyes. He refused to wear a coat or hat or gloves, electing instead to wear shorts even in arctic conditions. We began to get disapproving looks – and I'm sure it seemed like I was neglecting my child – but I simply could not make Sam wear his coat. It was easier to make him realise the consequences of his actions for himself than go into battle.

We found ourselves spending more time criticising and scolding him than focusing on the things he was doing well. Granny Mavis, with her wisdom and years of experience, was the first to pick up on these signs that all was not well with Sam, but we put it down to normal naughtiness. We'd heard all about the 'terrible twos' and assumed we were in their throes and that this phase would soon pass.

I was delighted to fall pregnant again.

Question marks

When Sam was around two and a half, he started at a private day nursery. It was a wonderful, warm, friendly environment. It had a big, bright hall that opened out onto a lovely safe and secure garden, complete with slides and a messy play area with water and sand. A separate quiet space meant the children could have their lunchtime nap in a peaceful snug. There were themed spaces dotted around, of dinosaurs or the seaside, which I knew Sam would love. Together with the nature walks in the local park, and the young, energetic and caring staff, it seemed to me like the perfect environment for him.

Suddenly, life became quite stressful.

By this time, I was working three days a week as an accountancy lecturer. Tony regularly worked long hours, and frequently travelled abroad on business. At weekends, he was a hands-on dad, and it was wonderful to see him and Sam together. But during the week, I sometimes felt like a single parent, as he was rarely home to put Sam to bed or help with the morning mayhem. I'd struggle to get Sam to nursery on time, arrive at work at an acceptable hour, and maintain at least a semi-professional air.

Going to work felt like a blessed relief from managing Sam's outbursts. These were increasing in frequency and intensity, and could be over anything – from the seam on his sock not fitting properly, to getting the Thomas the Tank Engine cup at breakfast instead of the Spongebob Squarepants one. Separating at the nursery gate was an experience I began to dread. Sam would work himself up into a hysterical mess and have to be peeled off me, yet the nursery always reported that once I had gone, he was fine. I felt the judgement of the other mothers on me as I rushed to drop him off and get to work on time. It was as anxiety inducing for me as it was for Sam, and I strongly felt working-parent guilt. I kept questioning whether it was healthy to leave him like this, or if I was damaging him by not being there for him around the clock. But if he was fine without me, as the nursery staff claimed, then perhaps he was manipulating me, and trying to make my life hard!

I also started to question whether his behaviour was 'normal', or if Granny Mavis had been right in her instinct that something more concerning might be underlying his antics. But I'd heard that lots of children have separation anxiety, so assumed he'd just grow out of it.

Instead, things only got worse. Birthday parties became a nightmare. While all the other children were able to sit and listen to the party entertainer, Sam would be running around doing his own thing. When he eventually joined in, he would act the clown to get attention from the other kids. At one party the following summer, Sam decided he was too hot, so without warning he stripped off his clothes and ran around naked! I was mortified. The other children found it hilarious, and Sam loved the attention, but I sensed the other parents looking on disapprovingly. On reflection, they may have pitied me.

This type of silly behaviour got the other children laughing, so he repeated it again and again. He had a formula that worked.

The intensity of emotions he showed and the impulsivity of many of his actions were bewildering to me. I had no point of reference to compare him to except the other children in our group, and it did seem to me that Sam was a bit different and more difficult than they were; but whenever I voiced my concerns to the parents, the response was a resounding 'You're worrying about nothing, he's only young!'

'It's a typical boy thing,' said one parent. 'They have so much energy, they're always messing around instead of listening.'

'My son was exactly the same at Sam's age!' said another. 'He'll grow out of it,' said a third.

There was one different voice at the time, though. A nursery friend, Pamela Wilson, came up to me one day when we were collecting the children.

'I was thinking about Sam's behaviour, as you seem to be so worried about it. Have you considered he might have a language processing issue?'

Pamela's daughter had learning difficulties, so she was right to suggest this, but my hackles rose. 'What do you mean he has language problems?' I snapped. 'Sam talks just fine – he obviously speaks well, and we've just had his hearing tested. The paediatrician said it's all good.'

It wasn't until much later that I realised language isn't just about talking or hearing, but is made up of many different elements. It became clear that the issues he had – running around doing his own thing instead of listening to what the entertainer was saying, refusing to follow instructions at home or at nursery, ignoring the teacher during tennis lessons and making up his own rules, or messing around when he was supposed to be reading a storybook – were not down to naughtiness, but rather problems with instruction processing, word recall and reading. These were all early signs that he had specific learning difficulties, but Tony and I had no real awareness or understanding of them at the time.

Sam, now twenty-two, remembers nursery as a happy period of his life. 'I felt very relaxed and cheerful during these early years,' he said to me recently. 'I have no memory of any issues. Nursery was all about unstructured play. There must have been lots of allowances made for me though.' He does, however, feel there is a correlation between behaviour and labels. 'As soon as you feel you may be different, then you no longer feel comfortable in your environment and you start acting up.'

As I was trying to make sense of Sam's behaviour, books about parenting began to pile up around my home. I was certainly making up for having dismissed all those baby books in the early years. Mary Sheedy Kurcinka's book *Raising Your Spirited Child* had a profound influence on me during this period. I was starting to understand that Sam's behaviour may be down to his nature, but if this were so, what could I do about it?

Later that year, we received notice that Sam had a place at the local state nursery. We had no hesitation in accepting it. The nursery was attached to a Church of England primary school, and a place there would mean Sam had a good chance of being accepted into that school in the reception year. These places were like gold dust (and still are), so we felt very fortunate to be offered what we saw as a golden opportunity to be in a wonderful community school with like-minded families.

Izzy's arrival

In February 1999, when Sam had just turned three, his little sister Izzy came into the world. It was a wonderful, natural birth, with no pain relief or instruments of torture. Within two hours of me arriving at hospital, Izzy popped out at a healthy 8 lb 4 oz (3.75 kg). (No more ten-pounders for me!) Everything – from my birthing experience to parenting her – was very, very different from what I had experienced with Sam.

At first, Sam was attentive and loving towards his sister. But as the days went on, his behaviour became unpredictable and there were times when I felt I could not leave them alone together. The tantrums and uncooperative behaviour escalated, and he started to have aggressive outbursts. His potty training took an about-turn. Not only did we have daytime and night-time wetting to deal with, but there were also episodes of soiling during the day. Every time this happened at nursery, I'd be handed a stinking plastic bag of his poo-covered clothes, and Sam would greet me at the gates in some other kid's sweatpants. I was advised to make Sam wash his own soiled clothes, but the battles that ensued often resulted in my just throwing them away. We went through a *lot* of value packs of underwear.

As we watched Izzy grow, we started to notice she walked and talked earlier than Sam had, and could play independently with her toys for sustained periods. She was curious about her surroundings, and was far less explosive and intense than Sam had been at the same age. She seemed robust and resilient, happy to get on with things, and settled quickly into any environment. In fact, everything about Izzy's development started to raise concerns in my mind about Sam and his progress. Nursery staff were reporting more and more often that he was boisterous, lively and shouted more than he talked. He gave up easily on tasks he found challenging and although he demonstrated an ability to concentrate at an age-appropriate level when he was interested in an activity, he could quickly become disengaged if he was unsure. He started to be more verbally aggressive and would even shout at strangers in the street.

Seeking help

Sam was now four years old and I, reluctantly, had begun to see that Pamela and Granny Mavis might have been wiser than I'd initially allowed myself to believe. A visit to my GP led to a referral to a local children's sleep and behaviour clinic, and the paediatrician there listened carefully and empathetically to my concerns. (She eventually worked with us on Sam's behaviour for the best part of a year.) At first, we went down the standard route, attempting star charts for every little achievement, and time-outs to calm him down. The star charts quickly descended into arguments over what needed to happen to earn the stars. Rewards were almost always delivered at weekends, which must have seemed so far away that they hardly counted as rewards at all. We took stars away for poor behaviour, which only put him off trying again. The time-out zone, at the bottom of the staircase, was really the naughty step and only served to increase his rebellious outbursts. The whole process was leaving us all feeling resentful and upset. It was only after four long months of fortnightly sessions – and after seeing how hard we were working on implementing her suggestions – that the paediatrician decided to refer Sam for:

- a developmental assessment;
- a speech and language therapy assessment; and
- an educational psychology assessment from the local education authority (LEA).

The journey of understanding Sam and his needs had entered the phase of professional involvement.

The request for this third assessment was refused. At the time, I took this to mean they did not consider Sam's behavioural issues serious enough to merit an assessment, but I realise now it was simply because of a lack of resources. I had no comprehension of the battle we were about to wage. We had entered what felt to us like a war and the enemy, sadly, was the very body that had been set up to ensure all children were able to access education and get the right level of support to enable them to progress in school.

Wading

A child with special educational needs (SEN) has a learning disability. This word, *disability*, is hard for many parents to accept, but it's defined in the *Oxford English Dictionary* as a 'physical or mental condition that limits a person's movements, senses, or activities' – so a disability is simply a limitation. Every one of us has different aptitudes! We might be slightly better at some things, slightly worse at other things.

For many of us, if we were to draw a profile of our aptitudes, it would look like the gentle rolling of the ocean waves, but a child with SEN would have a far more turbulent profile, with tsunami-like peaks and troughs as you move through the areas of aptitude. This is why many children with SEN are referred to as having a *spiky* profile. Sam's profile was spiky. It revealed an above-average IQ and a typical learning capacity, but crashed in certain cognitive areas. It was these troughs that were causing his issues in everyday living and in the classroom, and we'd been entirely unaware of them until this moment. If we couldn't see them, how would anyone else, and how could we expect them to understand?

I felt different to the other parents. I was in a different place to them, dealing with different issues. I was managing Sam, containing him, rather than mothering him. Surrounded by parents who appeared to be treating their children's progress as a project development exercise, with goals and targets, I felt as if I'd unwittingly entered some kind of race. While other mums were working with their children to develop fine pencil control and handwriting skills, it was a struggle for me to get Sam to sit at the kitchen table for five minutes without throwing crayons everywhere. And while other parents could take their children to the park and enjoy watching their carefree play, I was constantly on edge, wondering when Sam would snatch a toy or throw sand into another child's face. Surrounded by these parents and their children, I felt isolated and lonely. The guilt and responsibility

I felt were completely overwhelming. I was already failing and being left behind.

Searching online for some advice, I came across a short essay called 'Welcome to Holland', written just a few years earlier by Emily Perl Kingsley, describing her experience of having a son with a disability. She had been told that his condition would prevent him from having a meaningful life, yet he became an actor and has enjoyed a successful and varied career (even appearing on *Sesame Street*). 'Welcome to Holland' is a beautiful analogy from a parent who was surprised by disability in her child. It was not what she expected, but she learned to embrace it.

Welcome to Holland

I am often asked to describe the experience of raising a child with a disability – to try to help people who have not shared that unique experience to understand it, to imagine how it would feel. It's like this …

When you're going to have a baby, it's like planning a fabulous vacation trip – to Italy. You buy a bunch of guidebooks and make your wonderful plans. The Coliseum. The Michelangelo David. The gondolas in Venice. You may learn some handy phrases in Italian. It's all very exciting.

After months of eager anticipation, the day finally arrives. You pack your bags and off you go. Several hours later, the plane lands. The flight attendant comes in and says, 'Welcome to Holland.'

'Holland?!?' you say. 'What do you mean Holland?? I signed up for Italy! I'm supposed to be in Italy. All my life I've dreamed of going to Italy.'

But there's been a change in the flight plan. They've landed in Holland and there you must stay.

The important thing is that they haven't taken you to a horrible, disgusting, filthy place, full of pestilence, famine and disease. It's just a different place.

So you must go out and buy new guidebooks. And you must learn a whole new language. And you will meet a whole new group of people you would never have met.

It's just a different place. It's slower-paced than Italy, less flashy than Italy. But after you've been there for a while and you catch your breath, you look around … and you begin to notice that Holland has windmills … and Holland has tulips. Holland even has Rembrandts.

But everyone you know is busy coming and going from Italy … and they're all bragging about what a wonderful time they had there. And for the rest of your life, you will say 'Yes, that's where I was supposed to go. That's what I had planned.'

And the pain of that will never, ever, ever, ever go away … because the loss of that dream is a very very significant loss.

But … if you spend your life mourning the fact that you didn't get to Italy, you may never be free to enjoy the very special, the very lovely things … about Holland.

Emily Perl Kingsley

Melissa says: The importance of understanding your child

When we first become parents we transform from being the experts on child-rearing we were before we had any of our own to complete novices – without even an Allen key, let alone instructions. Raising children is a journey of discovery we take alongside them. At the same time as discovering what makes our individual children tick, we find out about ourselves. The more we understand about our children, the better our parenting, the more compassionate we can be and the more strategic our interventions. Children come in infinite varieties and there is no one-size-fits-all way to parent.

Elaine and Tony uncovered little pieces of the puzzle that was Sam as they went along. One of those pieces is temperament. Any parent with more than one child will know that all children are born with inbuilt, genetically determined personality traits; characteristics that define how they interact with the world. Some of these characteristics can be hard to live with when kids are young, but wishing they were otherwise won't make them so. And biology is not destiny – we can help our kids to understand their needs and shape their behaviour.

Sensitivity

Elaine talked about Sam's sensitivities. The first sign of these was his intense reaction to the man wearing a turban. Carol Stock Kranowitz describes reactions like this clearly in her book, *The Out-of-Sync Child*, explaining that this type of response arises from the brain's inability to correctly process sensory information – sights, sounds, touch, and so on. Some of this information seems to get 'stuck', and parts of the brain do not get the information they need to organise these stimuli into meaningful messages. This is sensory integration disorder (SID).

Even if your child doesn't have a sensory disorder, they may have a very sensitive temperament. Sensitive children feel emotions and experience stimuli through all their senses to a higher degree than others. This means that they can be overwhelmed in shopping malls and classrooms, and at parties, swimming pools and playgrounds. Socks really do feel unbearably scratchy and one brand of yoghurt tastes disgusting compared to another. They really will be able to smell things that you cannot. Constant stimulation can be exhausting and overwhelming and can lead to inappropriate behaviour such as Sam stripping off at the birthday party.

If you have a highly sensitive child you need to be aware of stimulation levels and do what you can to limit them. Sometimes that means taking your child away from an environment or giving them noise-cancelling headphones! You also need to be vigilant to protect their sleep.

These children will need lots of emotion coaching to help them put words to their big feelings (see Chapter 6). Being able to communicate with words is a better alternative to acting out in frustration.

Distractibility

Children, like Sam, who are very alert to stimuli, often have trouble prioritising information and they react to everything. They can get very distracted as there are so many external stimuli that capture their attention, and they need a lot of support to focus.

The parent of a distractible child learns to be an expert communicator, using a variety of methods including touch and other non-verbal forms of communication. This parent needs to give clear, brief, positive instructions in an intentional way.

Reactivity

Some children are cautious, while others leap right in and ask questions later. The cautious ones often pay close attention to detail. They may prefer to hang back and assess things, but will join in when they feel comfortable. Their first inclination may be to reject, which can be distressing or annoying for parents as their child declines food, gifts, outings, or even people. It can be embarrassing and you may worry about this glass-half-empty trait. While we do need to teach these kids socially acceptable ways of behaving, this analytical approach is not necessarily a bad thing. I really appreciated this characteristic in my own son when he was a teen, especially as his peers were engaging in really risky behaviour.

We can help children who dislike new things by preparing them ahead of time and coaching them on how to receive gifts and refuse food politely and have a go at things. Persist with presenting new things.

Adaptability

Change was hard for Sam. Moving from one activity to another was a real challenge for him and he would feel ambushed by the shift. You will know which of your children need to be told in advance what is going to happen (they need warnings five minutes before they have to stop playing and need help to find a stopping point in the game) and which ones will go with the flow. The slow-to-adapt ones will be the ones hanging on to your legs when you drop them off at nursery. Acknowledge how they feel and help them see how they can manage that anxious feeling. Direct them to the games/activities they enjoy. Give them lots of praise for steps towards independence, for being brave, or for using strategies to distract themselves.

Parents need to be aware of how many transitions these children have dealt with recently and how to accommodate them. When they moan about having to do homework they may need to transition from playtime to work time. Surprises (even nice ones) upset them. These kids thrive on charts and planners and family meetings to discuss what's going to happen. When they know what to expect, they feel more in control.

Intensity

Some children feel things intensely (they cannot *believe* you would give them the red plate rather than the blue plate), while others are more laid-back. The intense child feels all emotions strongly, so will explode with anger and frustration and feel that life is hugely unfair. But they will also feel great compassion and be very concerned about a wounded dog or a friend who's been left out.

An intense child needs help with feelings: acknowledge them without blame or judgement and show the child what to do with them. Model how you handle your own feelings – take some cool-down time when you feel upset, and engage in calming strategies such as doing physical activity, listening to music, making some art or going outdoors to get some fresh air. Demonstrate how to talk about feelings. Make sure you say, 'I feel hurt when you call me names like that. I guess you were really mad and I don't think you really meant it. Right now I feel a bit disrespected.' Don't say, 'You are so rude. How dare you talk to me like that!'

Persistence

Some children will nag until they wear you down, whereas others will accept 'No'. Some will give up easily, while others will stick to tasks until they've mastered them. Persistence is a great quality, unless what they're persisting with is arguing with you! Help your child see the good side of their character ('You didn't give up learning to ride your bike, did you? Now you can balance just fine!') and manage the more difficult aspects.

If we have persistent kids, we need to be very consistent as they will test the limits over and over – they need to see that the rules remain firm. We need to speak with clarity and conviction. It's OK to say 'No', but sometimes 'Yes, when ...' is better. We can help these kids climb down and move on from their current stance by describing their perspective. It takes two to battle – you can be the grown-up when you understand that your child needs help to let go. Brainstorming with your child not only helps them feel respected but also enables them to see that there is more than one way of doing things, ways that are acceptable to both of you. Help your child see that they can be a problem-solver.

Energy

Some children have phenomenal reserves of energy and can wear parents to a frazzle, while others will occupy themselves quietly or may even be quite difficult to enthuse. High-energy kids *need* to move. They learn and express themselves through their bodies. This energy can be great, but it sometimes needs directing. Plan for it by ensuring they have plenty of opportunities to move.

Communication should include gentle touch. Help them to calm their body down until they can hear you.

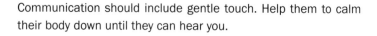

Parents of intense, sensitive, energetic, slow-to-adapt, persistent, negative, irregular, introverted or distractible children can help them to understand, appreciate and work with their personalities. Experience shapes the brain's physical structures, so we can help our children to adapt their behaviour and in doing so shape new neural pathways. We can change the way our kids are wired!

Life is much happier when we understand our children well. We can be calmer if we know what to expect and we can plan around the child's needs, whether these are temperamental, developmental, specific learning needs or needs arising from other conditions. We are not pandering to our children or indulging them. We are providing the optimal conditions for them to thrive. So it's up to us to observe carefully and research thoroughly to find out exactly what makes our kids tick.

At this stage, Elaine and Tony had little knowledge of how important understanding temperament was to parenting effectively. They knew Sam was super-sensitive, very impulsive and intense in his reaction to things, but had no idea that they could help with that.

Elaine's reflections

1. Understanding the stages of development can help parents have empathy, but children develop across a wide spectrum. Are you familiar with the general indicators of normal toddler development?

2. The arrival of a new sibling into the family can bring great joy, but can also highlight developmental differences. Have you found yourself comparing the

development of your children, and has it highlighted some key differences between them?

3. Understanding and accepting your child's temperament allows you to respond effectively to their needs. We can't change their temperament, but we can help them develop better responses. What is your child's temperament like?

4. There are many factors that affect parents' decision-making over which nursery school to choose. Sometimes a key concern is class size. What are the key factors for you in choosing a nursery?

5. A child with SEN has a learning disability. What connotations does the word disability have for you?

Further reading

Mary Sheedy Kurcinka, *Raising Your Spirited Child: A Guide for Parents Whose Child Is More Intense, Sensitive, Perceptive, Persistent, and Energetic*, 3rd edition, 2016.

Carol Stock Kranowitz, *The Out-of-Sync Child: Recognizing and Coping with Sensory Processing Disorder*, 2005.

3

Naughty, Stupid Little Child

(Primary School)

Misbehaviour and punishment are not opposites that cancel each other; on the contrary, they breed and reinforce each other.

Haim G. Ginott, *Between Parent and Child*

There is no question in my mind that children with learning difficulties suffer both educationally and socially. Unless the significant adults around them have sufficient knowledge, awareness and empathy, this can easily lead to low self-esteem which in turn can result in poor behaviour. Up to school age the early warning signs may well be there, but often don't fully reveal themselves till the child leaves nursery and starts 'big school', where more demands are placed on them.

When Sam started big school in September 2000, I had a hunch we may have already been en route to Holland. By the following June, we had definitely landed. The plane had touched down in a different location to where we had intended and we were woefully unprepared.

Rise and fall

I had been nervous about how Sam, and we, would cope with the transition from nursery school to reception. It's a milestone for anyone, but with Sam's behaviour becoming increasingly difficult to manage at home and at school, I felt a growing sense of anxiety. I had no idea what was around the corner. Was I worrying about nothing? Would he be compliant or were there going to be problems? Was it just that he was showing signs of delayed development, but would soon catch up?

Our original hope for primary school materialised – Sam was offered a place to stay on at the same Church of England school. By this time, though, Tony and I were firmly of the opinion that, as Sam was already struggling, we should really be looking to place him in a private setting. Class sizes would be smaller, he'd get more individual attention and tailored support from the teachers, and anyway, private education means better facilities and higher quality teaching ... right? We thought it was a wise and sensible decision.

We liked the look of a nearby school called The Grove. Classes were small and it backed onto a glorious common, an expanse of green open space and woodland, so we went to visit. Established some years previously with only a handful of pupils who had struggled to achieve their full potential in other educational environments, it was non-selective and attracted a wide range of families. The environment was unique and nurturing. They encouraged children and there was much fresh air and fun to be had. We were now aware that Sam might be an atypical learner, so the emphasis they placed on deep and meaningful learning in a fun and exciting way outside the classroom sounded perfect for him.

A plaque proudly displayed the school's ethos:

Every child has the right to be treated individually and uniquely, to be nurtured and encouraged according to his needs, to enable him to flourish.

And it had a farmyard on-site – a real farmyard, with sheep, chickens, ducks, pigs and goats! Sam was beside himself with excitement. We were all sold – this was the place where he would thrive.

Sam was content. The children went foraging on the common for acorns and conkers, fed lettuce to the rabbits in the farmyard, and before class would always have a good run around the playground to prepare themselves for learning.

The school's holistic approach was working, and Sam's confidence began to grow. He even wanted to get the school bus – on his own! My little boy! I initially felt he was much too young for such a level of autonomy until I realised it was me who wasn't ready for him to grow up. But Sam had emerged from the child who struggled to separate from me at the nursery gate to a brave and fiercely independent little boy. He got a taste of freedom and ran with it.

Today, Sam remembers the school fondly. 'I made some great friends there,' he tells me. 'There were lots of lovely walks on the common, and I loved feeding the farmyard animals. The best bit was the chocolate milk we got at break time,' he says with a smile. 'Birthdays were always great celebrations and every child could invite their parents to join them for lunch in the school dining hall. It was really good fun.'

The honeymoon period ended along with Sam's first term at The Grove. The school made allowances for the kids in the first term to let them settle in, but in the second term demands started to increase. The class teacher, Mrs Stone, implemented a rule that at the end of the day all the children had to line up, shake hands with her, make eye contact and say 'Goodbye, Mrs Stone'. Every day, Sam got one thing wrong. Sometimes, after waiting his turn, he would remember to shake hands, say 'Goodbye, Mrs Stone', but would look at the floor. Other times, he would look her straight in the eyes and give a firm handshake but stay absolutely silent. And on some occasions he'd get so nervous he wouldn't line up at all. I was frequently called in to speak to Mrs Stone at the end of the day. She would tell me, 'Sam was *most* disrespectful. He simply refused to comply with classroom rules. It won't be long before he's in Year 1 and it's really about time he stopped misbehaving like this.'

What we didn't appreciate at the time was that Sam wasn't meaning to be disrespectful or defiant. He was being faced with a four-part set of instructions to carry out simultaneously, and he just couldn't process the information. There is a widely held belief in our society that if we point out what a child gets wrong, they will change their behaviour. Yet in our case nothing could have been further from the truth. The more we criticised and nagged Sam about the importance of following this one school rule, the harder he found it. We were making it more and more difficult for him to succeed by adding to his stress.

By this point, the school had started having serious concerns about Sam's progress and suggested we try some learning support, and a gluten-free diet. Perhaps they had their reasons for putting him on a gluten-free diet, but this move was never explained. It seemed as though they were plucking ideas out of thin air.

Sam enjoyed the learning support. 'It was great fun – I got to leave the classroom and have one-to-one attention, which I loved.' As for the diet, 'That was ludicrous. It didn't change anything, it just made me feel different having to line up for the gluten-free pizza at school.' He reminds me that after being on this regime for six months, he devoured a whole loaf of white bread in one sitting. 'It was deeply satisfying.'

Farmyard chaos

Sam has always had a real love of animals. He used to spend as much time as he could playing with and tending to the animals at The Grove's school farmyard, although he'd often tell us how he thought they looked sad, all cooped up like that.

One morning, as he was approaching the end of his second term at the school, I gave Sam a kiss goodbye and he caught the bus as usual. I dropped Izzy off at her nursery and got the train to work, thinking about how it was always a joy to watch her skipping into nursery without a backward glance.

The next thing I knew, Tony was calling me from work, telling me the school had just phoned him. 'There's been a major incident. They're not coping well with Sam – they're saying he's getting increasingly angry.'

'What's happened?' I asked, trying to remain calm.

'They said he's done a really stupid, naughty thing.'

I could feel the panic rising in me. Has he got into a fight? Has he hurt one of the other kids? Has he …?

'He's let the animals out!'

Sam had opened the farmyard gate, and all the animals had headed straight out of the school and towards the frighteningly busy interchange nearby. There was mayhem as most of the school staff ran out to the road to round up the animals. Their heroically quick response narrowly prevented our five-year-old boy from being wholly responsible for causing chaos on one of the busiest roads in London.

From that day, the words *stupid* and *naughty* became killer words in the Halligan household. Sam became extremely sensitive to them, and saw red whenever anyone used them towards him. They had such a strong impact on him that we forbade the use of these words in our house. But there was no getting away from them – the labelling had started. Sam was branded a naughty boy by his peer group, by other parents and by staff. I felt ostracised and very alone. I didn't understand Sam's behaviour, but I knew he was not a bad boy.

Later, we finally got his side of the story. He'd got off the bus at school, found a hiding place, and lain in wait till everyone had gone inside for registration. He'd then walked calmly up to the farmyard. He wanted the animals to be free and happy and felt they should be living in the wild, and where better for their new home than the plains and woodland of the common. He'd even noticed a secret gate at the back of the farm to the school grounds. Everything had been planned – the animals would go through this gate, through the school, onto the common, and into freedom. The only issue was they hadn't migrated the way he'd planned.

41

Yes, his behaviour was atypical, to say the least, but he was so remorseful for what he'd done that I knew it wasn't out of malice. He was struggling. He understood the implications afterwards, but explained that he just couldn't help himself in the moment. It was as if the ancient, impulse-governing part of his brain had taken over from the rational part and controlled him. It didn't make him a bad person. There was just no pause button.

The head teacher called us to a meeting after the event. All I remember from this were the words, 'I suggest you migrate to specialist provision for autistic children.'

My world collapsed. It was the first time we'd heard the 'A' word mentioned in respect to Sam. Tony and I were stunned. It shook me like a thunderbolt. I felt winded, dumbstruck, panicked and overwhelmed, embarrassed and ashamed, and said nothing during the meeting. Were Tony and I to blame for what was happening? How could we place Sam in a school for children with autism when we didn't even know what we were dealing with? He had never been officially assessed or diagnosed.

Perhaps the school were just doing their best to let us know something was wrong, but they didn't have enough knowledge or experience to guide us properly or sensitively at that time. All they could see was that they were losing the battle with Sam.

We realised then that our preconceptions about state and private education in this country had been all wrong. It turns out the state education sector has a legal obligation to be inclusive, to work with all children and provide support to enable them to access education. The private sector, on the other hand, has no such obligation and if things get too difficult (and perhaps one or two of the more vocal parents complain loudly enough), they can ask you to leave.

We'd been cast adrift, all alone, left with no captain to steer the ship.

Sea of acronyms

I spoke to our family doctor, a wise and kindly man. 'Given the current situation,' he said, 'I'm going to refer you to CAMHS.'

'Kams?' I asked, blankly.

'CAMHS – Child and Adolescent Mental Health Services,' he replied. Even with his empathetic manner, the words 'mental health services' sent a shard of fear into us.

We soon found ourselves in the bustling centre of St George's Hospital, doctors and nurses swooping past us, unfamiliar beeps and bleeps coming from every corridor, the air thick with the smell of antiseptic and a heavy atmosphere of pathology as we followed the signs to our waiting area. Sam stayed close to me, quiet and frightened. As we got closer, the corridors became less busy, until we reached locked doors, buzzer access only, and a waiting room with a sad set of toys that looked neglected and uncared for. We had entered a system of scrutiny and diagnostic testing. Sam needed a developmental assessment, a speech and language therapy assessment, an educational psychology assessment and a psychometric assessment. He was screened and tested to within an inch of his life – and at such a young age.

Our first appointment was in the summer of 2001, and by the autumn we had a diagnosis. We sat and listened to the consultant psychiatrist: 'Sam has a pervasive developmental disorder. His problems are in the area of language and social communication. He has marked difficulties with peer relationships. His inability to understand his environment, which is partly masked by his apparently good verbal skills, leads to a high degree of frustration, low self-esteem and aggressive behaviour. Although he has some areas of functioning which seem to preclude the diagnosis, I believe on balance he meets the criteria for a diagnosis of Asperger's syndrome.'

We had the first label. Sam was on the autistic spectrum. But it was so off the mark to us. Even our local paediatrician, who had met with Sam a few times and was getting to know him, was surprised. 'Asperger's?' she exclaimed when we told her the news. 'I never would have predicted that diagnosis.'

Tony and I blindly accepted it. I printed off a little card from the National Autistic Society website, which children with Asperger's syndrome could carry around with them to show to others to explain some of their behaviour. As I read through the card, I didn't really think it described Sam. He wasn't 'gauche' or 'arrogant' or 'rude'. But it's what the experts had diagnosed, so it must be true. I started to doubt my own observations and my understanding of my own child. It added to my sense of powerlessness.

It was that diagnosis that prompted us, cap in hand, to approach Sam's previous school – the wonderful community school we'd removed him from the year before, having thought he'd be better off elsewhere. We were welcomed back with open arms. They listened to my story and knew immediately what needed to be done. The acronyms started flowing. They would set up an IEP (individual educational plan) for him and ask the LEA (local education authority) for a statutory assessment of his SEN (special educational needs) with the SENCO (special educational needs coordinator), who was wonderful. At last I felt we were in safe hands, in an educational environment that cared and understood, and that Sam would have a successful Year 1.

However, Sam doesn't have fond memories of this year. 'I just recall being in the spotlight and being asked to do things that I really could not do. Just being in the classroom environment and being asked to read out loud sent me into a hugely anxious state. I felt so vulnerable – and a real idiot – because I knew I was unable to keep up.'

The Biff, Chip and Kipper book series his classmates were progressing through had him stumped, his handwriting was illegible, and he rarely finished any project work, being unable to keep on task or organise his thoughts.

The pressure Sam felt at school was spilling into the home. Tony and I spoke about nothing except Sam, we were neglecting Izzy, and we felt close to breaking point. We were living in a constant state of stress and anxiety and we knew that additional resources were needed. Granny Mavis and Grandpa John were still living in Scotland, leading active and busy lives, but they always kept their promise and made time to come down and help out, giving us the odd respite break *sans les enfants*. Those weekends away were life-savers, but even though the children loved being with their grandparents, we never got off lightly when we came back. Sam's behaviour was always worse for the first twenty-four hours after our return.

It was at this time that we admitted our family needed some extra help.

We took the decision to hire an au pair: Annabel – a gutsy, in-your-face Antipodean with a hugely colourful personality. She arrived after answering our online advert for an English-speaking au pair to help with raising a high-energy six-year-old boy. Covered in tattoos and piercings, and with a penchant for climbing trees and skateboarding anywhere and everywhere, Annabel was a breath of fresh air, and just what our family needed.

Sam and Izzy adored her, and still do to this day. She's a highly sensitive and perceptive person. She loved taking the kids to the park, getting stuck in to their rough-and-tumble games, and bouncing on the trampoline. She had a really cool VW camper van, too. Sam developed an enduring love of cars in the hours and days they spent sitting in her camper outside the house having picnic teas. Annabel would tinker with the engine and Sam would watch and ask lots of questions. He was a happy chappy when there were no demands made of him, when he was free to follow his own agenda. While other children were engrossed in books or staring at screens, Sam was always at his best taking things apart and figuring out how they worked.

One evening, after I had tucked the kids into bed, Annabel and I sat down together. 'You adore them, don't you,' I remember her saying. 'I watch the way you gobble them both up at bath-and-bedtime. Your face glows as you snuggle them.'

I joined in, 'Snug as a bug in a rug.'

'It's so clear you'll do anything for Sam,' she continued. 'You trust other people for guidance and try so, so hard to do everything right.' She'd deduced that I had to trust someone else because the parenting methods I'd used from infancy were not helping Sam.

'It's like you've come to this place where you think you need to put your mothering instincts aside. You're parenting him *rationally*, following guidance from professionals. It must break your heart.'

Annabel was exactly right. My heart was breaking – and as for my parenting, it was a car crash waiting to happen. I no longer trusted myself. I felt so confused and bewildered by Sam's behaviour, which was escalating on a daily basis, especially at school. The school told us he had an anger problem, and that he was very aggressive. A support assistant in class, who was pregnant, feared for her own health and that of her unborn baby.

One day, I got a devastating phone call from school. Our worst fear had been realised – the police had been called. Sam had gone AWOL for three hours. As I felt the panic rising, I realised the teacher was telling me he'd been found safe and well.

'Where was he?' I asked, welling up with relief.

'In a cupboard!' the teacher replied.

Sam would adopt avoidance strategies whenever he found tasks difficult and started to do wilder and wackier things to avoid the spotlight on him. It was as if he was in a continuous state of fight-or-flight.

Sam recalls: 'I've got this weird memory of this cupboard. It was on the left-hand side of a classroom at the back of the school, overlooking the playground. I just wanted to get away, so I went into the cupboard and just sat there, listening to everyone in a state of panic looking for me. I then remember, after a very long time in there, just leaping out of the cupboard and saying, "*Surprise!*"'

At the same time as trying to avoid the teachers, Sam had become hard-wired to get attention from his classmates in any way he could. Negative attention was better than none and he was well versed at playing the clown. It was false bravado, an attempt to deflect attention from what he couldn't do, but we didn't realise this at the time. He would become the classroom entertainer and try to make the other kids laugh, but as his friends matured they started to see this behaviour as inappropriate. They began to distance themselves. As they withdrew, so did their parents. One day, I overheard a friend from our babysitting circle. 'I'm really glad Sam's not my son!' she clipped. I will never forget those words.

By spring 2002, the school admitted they couldn't cope, and the LEA suggested we place him in a more specialist environment. By then we'd had numerous educational psychologists visit Sam at school and give us advice, and we were fortunate enough to be seen by a senior officer, who was a highly experienced and compassionate man. It was clear, though, that mainstream education was not appropriate.

That autumn, when Sam was rising seven, we received a detailed neurodevelopmental report from a consultant developmental paediatrician at St George's Hospital. Her conclusion was insightful and, although not conclusive, provided an explanation that enabled us to understand more about Sam and his needs.

Her report read:

Despite Sam's lack of responses to discipline situations, he does seem to be articulating considerable distress at his predicament. He has made such comments as:

'You're not the boss of me'

'I just turn into a monster'

'I don't want to become a teenager because it will all just get harder and harder'

'I want a different brain'

Indeed, Sam was highly aware of his impulsive behaviour and was heartbreakingly remorseful after almost every episode. It was as if he was telling us he just couldn't help himself. Yet some of it appeared to be a manifestation of a self-fulfilling prophecy. One afternoon with Annabel, Sam and Izzy had been painting together. Without notice, Sam covered his hands in purple paint, jumped up and started smearing them on our walls, with purple splatters raining all over the furniture.

Annabel had clambered over the sofa to grab him. 'Sam, stop!'

'Why?' he'd cried, 'I'm a monster!' It was almost like he was only behaving the way others had labelled him.

The report continued:

> *I believe that Sam presents with a complex neurodevelopmental disorder, which has a number of constituent elements, all interrelated. I would agree that the primary diagnosis is that of an autistic spectrum disorder (also termed pervasive developmental disorder). However, Sam's emotional and behavioural responses are highly unusual and severe, and seem to stem from a very early onset of refusal and avoidance. This pattern of behaviour has been described by Professor Elizabeth Newson as pathological demand avoidance (PDA) syndrome. Although this term does not have universal recognition, I feel it helps to describe a particular behavioural pattern that requires a highly individualised and particular type of approach to management. I would consider it a subtype under the autistic spectrum umbrella. The cause of the extreme behaviour is felt to be anxiety.*

In addition to PDA, the report mentioned ADD (attention deficit disorder) and ODD (oppositional defiant disorder).

The specifics of each diagnosis had started to become a blur to us. The LEA suggested we look at schools for children with EBD (emotional and behavioural difficulties). The paediatrician went on to recommend trying medication: sertraline, a drug belonging to a group of antidepressants called SSRIs (selective serotonin reuptake inhibitors). Administering drugs to our child was a last resort for us, but Tony and I felt we'd come to the end of the road. We had no choice.

And so it was that we had a child with SID, PDA, ADD, ODD and EBD, who needed to be medicated with SSRIs.

Who was this Alphabet Kid, and where was our Sam?

Tribunal tribulations

Every parent of a child with SEN will come across people who become ambassadors for them. Pamela Wilson was my ambassador. We had many a meeting around her kitchen table where, with her insight, knowledge and wisdom, she helped open my eyes to the fact that Sam really did need specialist provision. And as he'd been thrown out of two schools in as many years, I listened to her intently. I was ready to consider anything! I was again at sea, almost a year on from the last time. But this time I was not so alone, and was starting to learn some captaining skills.

The LEA gave me a list of schools to visit. The first was one for children with moderate and severe learning difficulties, but the educational psychologist and the SENCO agreed this wasn't right for Sam. The second was a local state school with a unit for children with autism. One visit to the unit, where most of the children were non-verbal, confirmed this wasn't appropriate either. Sam's IQ was above average, and he had good expressive language, but had been identified as struggling with language processing. Where were the schools that could help him? The reality was that, back then, our borough had no schools suitable for Sam. Yet he was a kid in the 'syndrome mix', and was clearly not able to cope in a mainstream environment.

Pamela then introduced us to a specialist educational lawyer, who explained that Sam could access private specialist education in an environment suited to his needs, which would be paid for by the LEA. This sounded perfect! The lawyer identified a specialist speech and language therapy school on our doorstep – Pinewood School – which was run by a passionate head who had dedicated her life to helping children with speech difficulties. She assessed Sam and said he would be well suited to the environment. My heart sang! The lawyer stopped us before we could get too excited. He said we would have a fight on our hands as the provision's cost to the LEA was four times higher than that of mainstream schooling.

We presented the school to the LEA as a suitable placement but, unsurprisingly, the application was refused. It all boiled down to money. Getting Sam into this school was going to be stressful and ugly, but I was beyond determined to win. I was a lioness defending my cub.

We prepared up-to-date assessments from an educational psychologist, a speech and language therapist, and an occupational therapist. We'd enlisted them all as willing expert witnesses at the tribunal. The process of finding the right professionals, booking in the assessment, and preparing the background information forms ahead of the assessment was incredibly time-consuming by itself, not to mention the practical challenges of getting Sam to these professionals at times when he would be cooperative and compliant!

We spent day after day with the lawyer, preparing and scrutinising our evidence and detailing the minutiae of Sam's educational needs and the type of environment that would be best placed to serve him. I visited countless schools and had to compile a case for and against each one. The correspondence from the LEA formed an ever-growing pile of paperwork, and endless hours of our lives were spent poring over the statement, deciphering all the jargon, and reading every word, time and time again, to understand the difference between Section 5 and Section 6. It was a SEN jungle.

I had to prepare paperwork late into the night, while also preparing my lecture for the next day. I was multitasking between becoming an expert in SEN tribunals and lecturing on discounted cash flows and internal rates of return. My mind – and my life – was in chaos. Tony was getting burnt out from the stresses of work, and was coming home to the stresses of our family. Sam was all over the place, not happy at school, and getting more disruptive at home when demands were made of him. Izzy, on the other hand, bumbled along happily, not knowing any different.

Twenty-four hours before we went to tribunal, the LEA conceded. We'd spent thousands of pounds on legal and expert authority costs, and the stress had pushed us to near breaking point, but we'd done it. Okay, so we never got the chance to present our case, but by being prepared and not backing down we ensured that Sam could go to the best school for him.

In autumn 2002, we entered the new school, full of hope and optimism.

Drowning

We lasted eight weeks.

'It was a dark eight weeks,' recalls Sam.

Up until now all the schools and professionals had focused on Sam's poor behaviour, his quickness to anger, his impulsivity, his inability to focus and to follow instructions, his distractibility, and his intense reactions to things that did not go his way. Sam's agenda was almost always different from that of the adults around him, and he frequently became overwhelmed with despair, fear, panic. Tony and I had no idea how to deal with him. Our parenting pendulum was swinging from giving in and letting him run riot to being overly strict and dishing out punishments, and we had no comprehension of how to use a more positive form of discipline.

During his most recent assessments, Sam had been diagnosed with semantic pragmatic disorder. A child's communication skills rely on different elements of language development, and Sam struggled to master the 'semantic' skills (understanding and using the right meanings of words and phrases) and 'pragmatic' skills (knowing what to say when, and how to say it to other people). This meant he really laboured to get the meanings right when he learned new words and phrases, and often struggled with his memory recall in everyday speech. Pinewood School was for speech- and language-disordered kids, so it should have been perfect for Sam.

However, it all started to unravel very quickly. After just a couple of weeks, Sam was put on half-days only. The head, who was always so supportive, worriedly reported that when using time-outs it would often take three members of staff to contain Sam, who might then suddenly switch to calmness and return to class as if nothing had happened.

We struggled through the first six weeks. After the half-term break, it was a battle to get Sam to go back to school.

Sam remembers it vividly:

They couldn't deal with me in the classroom. As soon as I acted out, I would immediately be taken out of the classroom and put in this windowless room for solitary confinement. I felt as if I was locked in there for hours. It's not nice, because you're already really worked up and then you're thrown in this room with no windows and you can't get out – and it feels like the room's getting smaller and smaller. At first they had things in the confinement area – it was an old changing room, so there were benches and a bathroom. But I'd just trash everything. Then they took out all the furniture, so I'd trash the bathroom, and then they removed the toilet seat. They kept changing my environment, but didn't seem able to think of a better way to change my behaviour. It was pretty damaging. I've since read about criminals placed in solitary confinement and the profound psychological effects they suffer. I think it had a similar impact on me. It made me angrier and much more hypersensitive to external factors.

When Sam told me all this recently, it broke my heart. I'd known they were having trouble with him, but had been unaware how deeply unhappy it had made him. I'd been becoming less and less able to connect with Sam properly, and had even started to feel resentful of the amount of time all this was consuming. All my energy and attention was committed to ensuring this school was a successful placement. I couldn't have begun to imagine that this specialist provision, for which we'd fought so hard, would also fail, and in such a damaging way.

Immediately after half-term break, the LEA called an ad hoc 'progress review meeting' with the head teacher. Grabbing breakfast on the morning of the meeting, Tony and I chatted about an article in the paper reporting that the fire brigade were on strike that day. Then I dropped Sam off at school. Once again, he had to be prised from me, kicking and screaming. I left to catch my breath over a coffee and returned an hour later for the meeting. The head teacher, the educational psychologist, the LEA officer and I sat in the head's lovely office. For a moment, we basked in the sunlight streaming through the tall, Victorian windows, filling the room with warmth. 'Thank you all for coming,' said the head, and as she did, there was a riotous commotion outside the room. The fire alarm had gone off – this wasn't a drill, and staff and students were doing little to contain their panic. From the hallway, we heard the exasperated voice of a teacher shouting over the top of the furore, 'Oh my god, it's Sam Halligan again. He's set the fire alarm off!'

We then saw Sam (who knew he was in trouble) trying to make a quick getaway out of the front door and declaring to anyone within earshot, 'It's all right, the fire brigade are on strike today so nothing's going to happen! It's all going to be fine.'

The educational psychologist, who had been hearing only minutes earlier about how the school were not coping well with Sam's needs, broadcast to all, 'That child is not in the right environment. He has to go!'

....

I asked Sam later about his actions. He explained he'd just had to get out. He was overwhelmed every day he went to school, and would vigorously avoid demands that he found too taxing. Setting off the fire alarm got him out of class. He knew the fire brigade were on strike, so as far as this little six-and-a-half-year-old boy was aware, his actions wouldn't have serious consequences.

Except they did, and Sam could no longer stay at this school. It was time to move on again, but there was nowhere left to go. Sam could no longer access education in any conventional sense.

He could not be educated in school.

This realisation hit us hard. A couple of days later, I received a phone call from a friend who worked at our LEA. 'Elaine, is everything OK at home? I've just seen Sam's name on our list as a pupil missing from education.'

How had we arrived at this point? Were we the worst parents in the world? What were we getting so wrong that meant our beautiful, blue-eyed boy was now a social outcast? We felt the finger of blame heavily pointed in our direction, and the acute embarrassment and feeling of failure shadowed our everyday lives. Where do we go from here?

Sam understood the consequences. 'Yeah, it was a pretty low moment,' he recalls. 'After that, I was pretty screwed up.'

We were now in survival mode.

Melissa says: The importance of managing misbehaviour positively

Given how much the spotlight was on Sam, it's not surprising he started thinking, 'What's wrong with me?' Anything that contributes to a child's feelings of shame leads to insecurity and anxiety.

A diagnosis can be really helpful for the adults to understand what it is that the child needs, but we need to avoid pathologising them and adding to their shame.

Many of Sam's behaviours described in this chapter are the sort of thing that adults find infuriating. Even well-intentioned, kind adults who are normally calm and patient get exasperated when kids disrupt the class, refuse to follow instructions or rules, or show apparent defiance or rudeness, not to mention releasing animals onto a major road!

Even if adults stay calm, conventional wisdom would have it that when a child 'misbehaves' we should punish them. This is deeply ingrained in us. We feel if we don't do that, we are being soft or permissive.

But *punishment just doesn't work*, for anyone, let alone children who are having a hard time managing life.

Our goal is to teach children to behave well, to understand what is right and wrong, and to pass values onto them. But the only thing that punishment does is teach kids to avoid getting caught. They may cease an activity for fear of being punished, but don't learn the right way to behave.

Punishment is based on the assumption that kids mean to be bad, whereas children actually want to be good. The notion that if a child does something wrong we should do something unpleasant to them is revenge. It promotes feelings of resentment, rebelliousness and humiliation, and leads to loss of self-esteem and furtiveness.

Discipline, on the other hand, is about teaching.

All behaviour has a cause. Compare children's behaviour to pulling up weeds. If you don't get to the roots, the problem will recur.

The single most effective thing you can do when disciplining your child is to ask: what's feeding the 'misbehaviour'? Be curious when your child has done something inappropriate. We look for reasons to understand a behaviour, not to excuse it. We will still need to teach our children to behave in acceptable ways. Even if we don't immediately know what's causing a behaviour, this enquiry puts us in a more compassionate space and we are more likely to be effective if we work on the assumption that 'my child is doing the best he can, given what he's dealing with'. That may seem unlikely if you're assuming that your child is being defiant or manipulative or lazy. But there is often another way of looking at the same behaviour.

Sam's behaviour at his three schools had several related causes. His cognitive problems were in language processing and working memory, meaning he could not always follow instructions. He wasn't trying to be defiant. He used distraction techniques such as setting the fire alarm off to avoid doing what he found impossible. He didn't think he could succeed, so he lost motivation to try. His sensory processing difficulty meant that he was highly sensitive to his environment and his emotions. His temperament was also persistent, distractible and impulsive. When he freed the animals, he didn't mean to cause chaos, he just acted on his impulse to make them happy. He knew he was different and was fully aware that adults (and sometimes his peers) found him difficult. He felt he was unacceptable. His self-esteem suffered and he felt shame.

Shame is a very painful state. If a child feels like a bad person, it makes them want to hide. When my older son got in trouble a lot at school he felt so bad about himself he tried to escape that feeling by lying, blaming others or making excuses. Shame elevates stress and that feeling of not being good enough creates anger and controlling, impulsive behaviours. It can be triggered very easily, say by a disapproving look. We can see that much of Sam's behaviour was caused by his feelings of shame.

When we know what conditions our children are operating under we can be more empathetic, and it allows us to give them the support they need. You will see as Elaine's story unfolds how she did just that.

What are some other reasons for poor behaviour?

Expected behaviours

Sometimes the reasons are simple. The child may just be tired, bored, hungry, unwell or curious. Sometimes a behaviour is just what you'd expect for that age, such as when a four-year-old squeezes all the toothpaste out of the tube in order to hear it squelch (they don't mean to be wasteful or destructive) or when a twelve-year-old wants to use their tablet more than you allow (they're following a compulsion, not trying to be defiant). Other times the behaviour is as a result of temperamental traits. Introverts may find a busy classroom overwhelming and seek respite in the library. Reactive kids reject new experiences.

They need attention

Children learn that it is easier to get attention for negative behaviour than for positive behaviour because we usually pay more attention when they are behaving badly than when they are behaving well.

They're full of emotions

Many inappropriate behaviours have at their root anger, disappointment, frustration, inadequacy, jealousy, isolation, powerlessness, confusion, loss, shame, feeling overwhelmed, a lack of control, etc. Stress contributes to hyper-arousal, aggressive responses, impaired executive functions such as memory and organisation, and difficulty with impulse control and can make children fidgety. Children may act out if they can't say what they need.

They're living in the moment

Young children have a very different tempo to adults. They can get absorbed and don't seem to have any sense of urgency, or may find it difficult to wait.

They're immature

Their lack of experience and their brain's underdeveloped frontal lobes mean they are impulsive, forgetful, have poor self-control and lack judgement. They find it hard to manage their feelings and delayed gratification is difficult for them. This is heightened when children have continued stressful experiences, as Sam did.

They have a different agenda

Children have their own priorities. You want to get out of the house on time with everyone dressed, breakfasted and with all relevant kit. They may want to read a book, play with a toy, save their hero from the monster, or daydream.

They don't understand

Sometimes we assume that our kids know what's expected of them, but in fact they might not understand what to do or how to do it. Or they might think the task is too difficult for them. There may be too many instructions at once. Young children can only hold a few pieces of information in short-term memory.

They identify as 'naughty'

When Sam misbehaved at school, the killer labels of 'stupid' and 'naughty' were used. He built up an image of himself as being the naughty boy, which started a self-fulfilling prophecy.

....

So what can parents do?

1. *Give lots of attention for the good things your child does.* We get more of what we pay attention to. Look for small examples – 'You looked at me when I was talking. That's polite.' 'Even though you didn't think you liked green peppers, you had a taste. That was brave.' 'Thank you for putting your clothes in the laundry basket when I asked you to. You can be a cooperative boy.' This teaches them that they can get attention positively. Change their self-perception by painting a picture of them as being good and capable. Also just delight in them and let them know how much you value them just for being themselves. 'I love the way you show how happy you are by jumping high.'

2. *A positive relationship is the foundation for any discipline.* Spend fun time with your child.

3. Teach children to manage their emotions by *acknowledging their feelings and coaching them* in what to do with them. Acknowledge their desire to do what they want, as well as any resistance to what you're asking them to do. Empathise when something is difficult or boring, and give them a reason for doing it. When a child feels understood it enables them to express remorse.

4. Have *realistic expectations* of your child. What's reasonable to expect of them at their age, with their temperament and their specific needs? This means you need to be well informed about any condition your child may have.

5. Give them *appropriate levels of power*. Where can they have choices? Maybe they can't choose *whether* to brush their teeth, but they could choose where, when and how.

6. *Give few, clear, simple instructions framed as positive directions.* Use authoritative words and body language.

7. Provide clear, consistent and *positively framed rules and routines*. Write them down or have picture charts. Acknowledge when they follow them. When they can't do something, help them get it right, don't punish them.

8. When something goes wrong:

    a. If necessary, take *immediate action to prevent harm* to people or things.

    b. Everybody take some *cool-down time*.

    c. *Connect with your child* by acknowledging the feelings that led to the behaviour.

    d. *Problem-solve.* Get your child's input – work out how to make amends and what to do differently next time.

Elaine's reflections

1. Starting 'big school' is a key milestone in a child's life. Are you concerned about how your child will cope?

2. A diagnosis can be important in helping you understand and be empathetic to your child's behaviour. If your child has been diagnosed, was it helpful or did it add to your sense of powerlessness?

3. For some children, they learn that it is easier to get attention for negative behaviour than for positive behaviour. Have you fallen into the trap of focusing too heavily on what they are getting wrong?

4. All behaviour has a cause. What do you think is behind your child's misbehaviour?

5. Positive discipline, delivered calmly, is designed to help children learn how to behave without losing self-esteem. Punishment is often delivered in anger and with criticism, and makes a child feel bad. Can you think of examples where you have punished your child and the behaviour has worsened?

Further reading

Haim G. Ginott, *Between Parent and Child: The Bestselling Classic That Revolutionized Parent–Child Communication*, 2003.

Daniel J. Siegel and Tina Payne Bryson, *No Drama Discipline: The Whole-Brain Way to Calm the Chaos and Nurture Your Child's Developing Mind*, 2014.

4

There Has to Be Another Way

(Out of School)

The power of influence is greater than the influence of power.

**Attributed to Michael Grinder,
communications expert**

After just a few weeks on a drug called sertraline, Sam was playing with Izzy and me in the park opposite our house, crunching about in fallen leaves. I noticed how well Sam was getting on with Izzy, having finally allowed myself to think that perhaps we had made the right decision by medicating him. And then he turned to me, looking dazed. 'Mum ... I feel spaced out ... I feel like I'm having an out-of-body experience.' In that moment, every cell in my body was screaming that this was just not right for Sam. I felt instinctively that there had to be another way. In our household, where you will struggle to locate a paracetamol tablet, medicating my child did not sit comfortably with me. But on everyone's advice, we continued with it. After all, we were not the experts in this field, and we felt we needed to trust the professionals.

Painful lessons

At every step of the way in helping your different or difficult children, you will meet significant people who have an important impact on your decisions and help you gain clarity on what to do next. At this step, I met Sue Kumleben, who would later become an integral member of The Parent Practice team. We were introduced by a mutual friend, who spoke passionately about Sue and her experiences. Sue also had a son who'd struggled in mainstream education, but she was seeing excellent results with a technique they were employing. She generously agreed to speak to me to discuss her approach and share with me the actions they were taking. So, late one November evening, once the children were in bed, Sue and I spoke on the phone for what ended up being a full hour. That hour turned out to be truly life-changing.

It was the next turning point in our quest to help Sam access education. She described her son's needs and the remarkable help she was getting from a behaviour modification centre in London. I hadn't heard of anything like this before, but Sue was evangelical about the transformative results. I needed no further encouragement. If we had to have some time away from normal education, so be it. In fact, education became the last thing on my mind at this time, as I knew that in order for us to function as a family, and ensure Sam stayed out of prison, we had to adopt some radical methods. This is the point where we, as a family, had to completely recalibrate what was normal.

We started Sam at the Hawthornes Centre in the first week of 2003, funded entirely by our LEA. The financial support came as a great relief to us because my part-time job as an accountancy lecturer was becoming increasingly untenable as I juggled the demands of our atypical family. Tony, whose job had been taking him abroad for weeks at a time, could see what I was going through. Although the long-haul travel was taking its toll on him, he thrived on his job and was at the top of his career. But at this point, he made an extraordinary, selfless decision, and resigned from his job. He had been with the company for thirteen years, having arrived there fresh off the boat from South Africa as a temp. He had no idea what this decision would mean for his future career, but he wanted to be at home to support us all emotionally. I fully appreciate that not everyone is as fortunate to have such a supportive partner. I adore him for that decision.

Looking back, I can see that turning away from traditional education and undertaking an intensive behaviour modification programme was an extreme action to take. But we were at a very vulnerable point in our lives. As parents, we do the best job we can with the resources we have, and at that time, my emotional resources were exhausted.

The Hawthornes Centre was not like any normal school. It operated from a small terraced Georgian townhouse on a peaceful, tree-lined street in west London. On the first day, Sam, Tony and I walked up to it in subdued, curious silence, apprehensive about what was to come. Entering through the little squeaky gate into the front garden, it felt like we were just visiting someone's house, but once the front door opened it became clear that this was no cosy family home but a functional working environment. We were met by a rather stern and unsmiling woman, who introduced herself as the director. She wore a large badge with her name on it. All the staff wore name badges, and insisted everyone on-site did so too. It was formal and a bit intimidating.

I peered behind her and saw a narrow corridor leading down to the back of the building. The walls were bare, and the ceiling held a solitary light bulb. At the back, a garden housed a trampoline. The atmosphere felt austere but I consoled myself with the thought that the staff were experts in behaviour management.

As we were led inside, I noticed a landing leading into a rabbit warren of little rooms – bedrooms that had been turned into teaching spaces.

It was to become our home from home for the foreseeable future. I became intimately familiar with the local shops, library and community spaces as I made the daily commute from south London and spent most of my days either in or near the centre. For Sam, the trampoline in the garden would become a lifeline, as he spent much time there calming down or working off his high energy levels.

We were led into a large room, which had a bit more life in it than the hallway, with pictures on the walls and toys scattered around the floor. Two teachers and a support assistant were waiting for us. After an initial chat, they invited Sam to play a board game with them. In typical fashion, he kicked up a fuss.

'I'm not playing. It's stupid. I want to leave,' he said. Normally we would have just let him, as other experts had told us that children with PDA must be approached non-confrontationally. But on this occasion, he wasn't allowed to do what he wanted to do. He emptied a rubbish bin defiantly.

'Sam, can you pick that up, please,' said one of the teachers. Sam shook his head, started to kick out at the teacher and made to leave the room. Within moments two adults were restraining him, face down on the floor. Tony and I stood watching, open-jawed, stunned by what had just happened. We felt powerless to come to Sam's defence. These were the professionals, they were our lifeline, the experts in behaviour management. But I also felt intimidated. Tony and I glanced at each other, and his face revealed he felt the same. We looked back to the two adults restraining our slight young son, pressed down on the floor. When the staff saw us staring, the support assistant explained that restraint was a reasonable consequence in this situation.

This scene didn't feel right. But as we had nowhere else to go, and were among experts, we just stood and watched.

On the second visit, Tony wasn't with me, and the same thing happened. But this time, as there was only one other adult there, I was told I had to sit on my child's legs and restrain him myself. I had no training, no real understanding of the implications or consequences. I instinctively felt that what I was being asked to do was not right. It was like breaking in a wild horse. This was surely a violation of a child's rights. It was as if I had lost the ability to think rationally and logically and was unable to find my voice. No child should ever be restrained as a punishment and yet I had allowed it to happen.

I slept badly that night. The next day, I had more strength to speak the director. Authoritarian and overbearing, she exuded control. I was in awe of her. She held the golden ticket to Sam's future.

I began: 'I feel I was put in an …' – I chose my words carefully – 'unfortunate situation yesterday.' We sat down in her office and I explained what happened. 'I really don't think it would have ended up that way if the right number of adults had been on-site. Also, I'm worried what emotional implications this experience will have on my son. I'm no psychologist, but from his reactions yesterday and his behaviour today I can't help but feel—'

'Thank you for telling me your thoughts,' she cut in, and with that, she stood to show me the door.

'How bizarre,' I thought. No discussion, no explanation. She seemed to have interpreted my comments as unwelcome criticism. But having explained my position, I felt better – stronger, empowered. From that point on I was able to cherry-pick the behaviour modifications that worked for us and disregard the rest.

The restraint policy was used at the centre with other children too. A dear friend of mine later attended the centre with her husband and four-year-old son. She'd told me that during their first visit, as they'd waited timidly in the corridor to meet the director, a teacher had come racing out of one of the rooms. 'You, come and help me,' he'd demanded, gesturing to her husband. 'A boy needs to be restrained.' So their first experience of the centre was holding down someone else's child. This had made them uncomfortable, but, like us, they felt powerless; what could they do but listen to the experts?

I soon learned to select the techniques I was more comfortable with to use at home, and restraint was not one of these techniques. With the benefit of hindsight, I can now see clearly that Sam, who was already consumed with fear, pain and overwhelmedness, became initially more explosive and aggressive due to repeatedly being restrained at the centre. For Sam the damage had been done. He remembers everything about the centre.

The move there made me even angrier. My relationship with education was so damaged by then that I felt they were tricking me into being educated, by playing board games in this sterile environment. This place was known as a school, but really it was just a house, with fire doors everywhere. There was so little space. There were four of us there, and we were all completely different from one another. One was older and had severe cerebral palsy, which was quite debilitating. Another guy, whose father was a footballer, had ADHD. I could relate to him a bit more, but he was hard to get on with. The third lad was quite autistic and had a fascination with battle re-enactments. I had absolutely nothing in common with any of them. I felt isolated, and felt strongly that I was not in the right place.

I don't blame Mum and Dad for putting me there, but I do think they made a big mistake. The environment was really weird, controlling and abusive. Being out of school was quite damaging for me. I lost a lot of social skills. But I know it was the right thing for my parents to do at the time. I know that was an important time for Mum and Dad to try and get me accessing some form of education. I still believe I was exposed to an environment that wasn't appropriate, though. I was really misunderstood.

For me, the worst part is that my experience there made my anger worse, taught me aggression, which was not good. But my parents were holding on for dear life, doing whatever it took. I recognise that they were being completely selfless and, at the time, it may have seemed like the right thing to do. I believe it set me back considerably, though. It took me a long time to get over it.

Sam finds it difficult to talk about his experiences at the centre. When he does, his memories unearth so many emotions for us all, ranging from enormous guilt to extreme distress.

Things got worse before they got better. But they did get better, and, despite our harrowing experience, we saw it through.

The approach at the Hawthornes Centre towards children with PDA was the antithesis of everything we'd been taught up to this point. Here, boundaries and firmness were good. They maintained that children need rules and must do what they're told. Despite some aspects that I didn't like at the time and now think amounted to mistreatment, we were also introduced to many positive skills. However hard it was for Sam and for all of us, I firmly believe it was the gateway to learning about positive parenting.

It was while Sam was at Hawthornes that we met Melissa, who was our family support worker. Every week, as part of the programme, we visited her home to be educated in how to be more effective parents. She coached us in the importance of forging positive connections with Sam by noticing the positives in his behaviour. This would help improve his self-esteem and cooperation. And so we started the arduous process of learning a language that was entirely new to us: descriptive praise. We had to describe what Sam was doing, positively. It's different from conventional, empty, evaluative praise ('clever boy', 'awesome', 'good job'), which is easy to throw over your shoulder without much effort. And children often don't believe it. Descriptive praise takes more time, more careful observation, more attention. But it is specific, genuine and credible.

We were taught to notice the small things (and I mean small) that he was doing that were good – or even just not bad – and to mention our observations to him. When you point out to your children what they're doing right, and perhaps explain why it's a good thing, they will believe it. Importantly, they will absorb it as part of their identity.

It wasn't until then that I realised the tremendous power that words can have in raising a person's self-worth, even from rock bottom. With Melissa's help, we remained open-minded, gained the courage to try new approaches, and watched as these positive parenting techniques we were learning worked their magic.

Within two months, Sam had started to make progress. He was beginning to accept his abilities and, for the first time, was motivated to learn. Slowly but surely, we started to see glimmers of a compliant, loving, empathetic, sensitive, helpful, wonderful little boy. We had not been able to see any of this before.

....

It was around this time that Annabel announced she would be moving on. She was heading back to Australia to train as a teacher. It was so hard to see her go. She handed me a beautiful, powerful letter before she left. In it, she'd written:

This year with your family has changed the direction of my adult life, and has changed me, and you have played a huge part in that. Thank you. It will break my heart to leave because it's not only Sam and Izzy whom I love dearly, but you also. You have been a true friend to me and shown more support than I could ever have imagined.

I didn't know what we'd do without her. But before she left, in her usual efficient and proactive way, she offered to place an advert online and help me recruit our next au pair. Within a week, she found Hayley, fresh from Durban, on the east coast of South Africa.

Energetic and vibrant, gutsy and hard-working, Hayley's wisdom and experience belied her seventeen years. Where Annabel had been at home on her skateboard, Hayley was at home out on her surfboard, and looked the part too; a tall, strawberry-blonde figure carving through the waves.

Sam immediately took to her. On her first day, before she'd barely set down her suitcase, a trampoline was delivered to the house and within five hours she had it erected and ready to go. Assembling home gym equipment had been nowhere in the job description, but she'd started as she meant to go on. Nothing fazed her. She was another huge help to us, playing combined roles of live-in au pair and learning support assistant, and accompanied Sam every day on the train to the Hawthornes Centre.

With the enhanced communication and connection skills we were learning, and by working as a united front with Hayley to ensure consistency, Tony and I slowly started to get back in charge while we gained a greater understanding of Sam's temperament and the reasons underlying his behaviour.

A weight is lifted

One fascinating insight we got at the centre was that during the whole time Sam's behaviour was so challenging, it had been almost impossible for teachers and professionals to diagnose his specific learning issues. But once his behaviour started to improve, he began to feel better about himself, his sense of self-worth increased, and it then became clear to the teachers that he was showing all the signs of being dyslexic.

There was a marked discrepancy between Sam's intellectual capacity and his ability to spell, read, decode phonics and write, but up until now, no one had been able to see this under his behaviour. The signs that now began to show indicated a poor working memory (which suggested phonological deficit, meaning he had trouble decoding and processing speech) and dyspraxic-type difficulties such as large, ungainly handwriting. Sam had undertaken so much intensive diagnostic assessment over the past couple of years that we decided not to pursue a formal diagnosis at this point – but once dyslexia had been suggested, everything seemed to fall into place. When we did commission another educational psychology report a couple of years later, it showed that Sam still had sensory issues but the overarching diagnosis was, indeed, that he had severe dyslexia.

It was the most enormous relief to have an explanation for his behaviour. Sam's constant frustration caused by his inability to read and write like the rest of his peer group had made him feel overwhelmed and anxious.

So many parents are fearful of a diagnosis in case their child is stigmatised. But to us, having this diagnosis was immensely helpful. Sam is dyslexic, and always will be. But rather than the dyslexia defining him, he now knows more about how he learns, and can play to his strengths to maximise his potential. Realising that neither we, nor Sam, were to blame was a life-changing moment for me and Tony. With this new awareness, we could finally work with Sam, support him, and fully understand his educational and emotional needs.

One step forward

Despite the changes we were making by adopting positive parenting techniques, we were still on an emotional rollercoaster ride. Although Sam's explosive outbursts were becoming less frequent, they were also becoming increasingly dramatic, and often seemed to appear from nowhere.

One day I was shopping in town with him and Izzy; we popped into a chemist for a few things and Sam saw some snacks near the till.

'Mummy, can I have a bag of crisps, please?'

'No, darling, we're about to have lunch.'

'Please?'

'No.'

'Pleeease?'

'No, Sam, we're just about to—'

And without warning, he exploded, turning to the nearest shelf and swiping all the bottles of shampoo and hairspray and lotions and potions onto the floor, while shouting at the top of his lungs, 'You're the worst mother in the world! I want to put you in the rubbish bin!'

It was complete carnage. Izzy was frightened and burst into tears. In my panic I resorted to restraining Sam using the same awful technique I'd objected to when we'd started at the Hawthornes Centre. With the three of us there on the floor, among all the bottles that had scattered everywhere, I felt publicly humiliated as the other shoppers fell into a stunned silence. It was a new low. In fact, Melissa often talks with compassion and humour about low parenting moments – she calls them 'LPMs'. The worst ones are often in a public place, where you have a child doing something embarrassing like having a tantrum and an audience gathers, watching and judging silently. This fit the bill exactly.

Sam's outbursts were also getting aggressive. They affected not only our lives but those of family and friends around us, too. The shame and humiliation we felt, knowing our child's behaviour was affecting the lives of others, was excruciating. One day in Wimbledon Park, we'd spent the afternoon playing crazy golf. We'd had a lovely, relaxed time. When it was approaching time to go, I let Sam know, giving him five minutes to take a couple more swings and gather his things.

But when the five minutes were up, Sam didn't want to leave. He ignored my requests, refusing to put down the little club and running off when I approached him. I tried to shake off the grip of frustration that was taking hold. I'd done everything possible to ensure we'd had a successful afternoon, and felt it wasn't unrealistic to expect Sam to do his bit and leave the park when asked. But asking fell on deaf ears. He was now in full-on uncooperative mode, and before I knew what I was saying I'd resorted to blackmail: 'If you don't come with me right now, we will not come back and play golf again.'

I knew it wouldn't work, but my button had been pressed. Predictably, Sam went into meltdown.

At that moment, my friend Gail arrived with her son. She saw I was struggling and that Izzy was getting upset, so she offered to speak to Sam. In a flash, he whipped out a penknife, brandishing it at the four of us, and threatened to kill us. His eyes and lips were tight with fury. It was beyond anything we'd ever expected to happen. We froze.

Gail instinctively pushed her son out of harm's way and started speaking. She looked calm, but there was a frightened tone in her voice I hadn't heard before. She drew on every technique she'd learned. 'Sam, well done for stopping there and not doing anything silly with that knife. You're showing self-control, which is really good. I know you; I know you understand the difference between right and wrong, and I know that you don't harm people.'

Sam broke down in tears and handed me the knife. He was immediately remorseful and anxious to show us (and himself) in any way possible that he wasn't a monster. He helped pack up our things, carried a bag, and held his sister's hand as we walked home.

Gail later told me she knew she had to stay calm, but confessed her legs had gone to jelly. She was also acutely aware that had she tackled Sam physically and tried to get the knife out of his hand, things could have gone very wrong.

Having read about the side effects of SSRI drugs, and that there was some controversy surrounding their effects on suicidal behaviour, these episodes began to ring alarm bells for us. Worried that it might be Sam's medication that was exacerbating his mood swings, we raised our concerns with his paediatrician. To our immense relief, she agreed that the drugs no longer appeared to be improving Sam's behaviour, and we started the process of weaning him off them.

With hindsight I now realise these explosive episodes were probably due to a combination of the drugs' effects and the impact of being repeatedly restrained at Hawthornes. It was our biggest mistake, allowing this restraint to happen. Sam had been physically controlled and we had been emotionally controlled. Thank goodness the positive parenting strategies replaced coercion.

Sam spent eighteen turbulent months at the Hawthornes Centre. It became ever clearer to us that we had been too critical of him in the past, focusing on his negative behaviour instead of the positive things he did. ('Sam, why can't you just behave like a normal child?' 'Why are you doing that? Just calm yourself down.' 'Your sister's not making a fuss, and she's younger than you.' 'What's wrong with you?') In contrast, the centre's methodology to help Sam achieve his potential – behaviourally, academically, socially and emotionally – followed a consistent approach of being positive: absolutely no criticism, scolding, telling off, nagging, lecturing or threatening. We also learned how to be firm, to be clear about the use of rules, rewards and consequences, and how important it was for both of us to be consistent – to work from the same song sheet. The training was not just for Sam, but also for me and Tony. It was an intense and time-consuming commitment. During term-time, I had to attend the centre with Sam every day and observe the skills being used; and every week, all four of us attended an hour-long family session with Melissa and Tony and I had additional ninety-minute parent sessions. It was all-encompassing, all-consuming, and it was our life. Not only was the commitment emotionally and physically exhausting, we also often found it confusing getting 'back in charge' and learning, almost from scratch, how to connect and communicate effectively. We were not going to give up now, but we faced many more lows.

One cold evening, Sam and I were returning home from the centre after another long day, running to catch the rush-hour train. The 16:58 service must have been one of the busiest trains in the country. It was truly unpleasant and, at times, felt dangerously overcrowded. Sam was stressed, exhausted, hungry and overwhelmed. We were lucky enough to grab a couple of seats before everyone else piled onto the train. Soon the carriage became a solid mass of bodies pressed up against each other, everyone tired and tetchy and wanting to get home.

Sam started kicking one of the passengers standing beside him. I asked him to stop, but he continued. Suddenly I started to feel overwhelmed too. I was in a crowded carriage and it was obvious I could not control my little boy. He was clearly aggressive and dysfunctional and I was unable to stop him. I reprimanded him. I threatened him. I nagged him, and begged him, but his behaviour got worse. Understandably, the lady who was under attack from Sam was getting increasingly upset, her tuts and huffs getting louder and more hostile until suddenly, at full volume: 'What your boy needs is discipline – a darned good smack will sort him out.'

I felt hopeless, embarrassed, and completely out of control. I didn't know what to do and then out of nowhere, on this packed London train (where so much as engaging eye contact with other passengers is frowned upon), I heard myself making a speech: 'My child is autistic. I need your support, not judgement, as I am dealing with a disabled child.' I went on, now channelling Bonnie Harris, author of *When Your Kids Push Your Buttons*: 'He is not being a problem, but having a problem. As you can see, I am not coping well, but the last thing in the world I am going to do is to smack my child for having a problem. Will you all please stop judging me and will someone help me to leave the train at the next station.'

The silence was excruciating.

Then another passenger spoke out. 'Yeah, leave that poor lady alone – she's doing the best job she can.' And in an instant, the whole carriage descended into a heated argument about how to discipline a child, whether I was doing it right or wrong, how little we understand about autism, and whether or not smacking is an effective form of discipline. Sam sat wide-eyed and silent as he observed all the adults around him behave like they were having a playground slanging match.

We got off the train at the next station. I realised we were still miles from home. I sat on a bench on the platform and I wept. Sam was quiet, meek as a lamb, and comforted me as he realised the impact of his own behaviour on others around him. This was my lowest LPM.

....

Not long after the train incident came a breakthrough. Once again, after an exhausting day, Sam started acting up at the station on the way home. This time, he ran away from me. My heart stopped as he sprinted off across the railway bridge and hid behind a bench on the platform across the tracks. Hawthornes had taught us that being in charge meant that when a child ran away, you were not to chase unless there was a serious risk to health or safety. In that fleeting moment, I did my risk assessment, and concluded Sam was safe on the platform where I could see him.

So this time I sat it out, waiting. I read my newspaper, watching him out of the corner of my eye as he tried to play this cat-and-mouse game. I realised I was breaking a deeply ingrained pattern of behaviour. It took courage and will-power (and a huge degree of trust that Sam would not actually do anything stupid) but, for the first time, I was letting Sam know he was no longer controlling this merry dance.

After a while, I went over to the opposite platform and asked Sam if he felt ready to come home. He looked relieved that I was not shouting or angry. This allowed me to calmly coach him, using the language we'd been taught over the past few months. 'I understand that you must have felt very angry with me when you ran to the other side of the platform,' I said in my best coaching voice. 'You've been making so much progress with being responsible and mature, so something really significant must have been bothering you that made you do what you did.' And then it all came out. He told me about how he'd had a really bad day at the centre. His remorse and embarrassment were evident, and he admitted he'd bitten the teacher in a fit of rage. He said (again) that he hated the centre. Then, he told me something that made me feel queasy. *The teacher had bitten him back.*

'She said it was to teach me a lesson,' said Sam, quietly.

Today, Sam is adamant that the environment we placed him in made him angrier. 'I think it made me quite violent, and that's the part I regret. I feel so sad now about how angry I got, and I know how much that hurt you,' he told me when we discussed this moment recently. 'I also remember pushing

Dad over one day in a fit of rage. His face was so full of shock. I hated myself for what I did.'

For Sam, this was his lowest moment in his childhood. Tony and I didn't know what else to do. Giving up at this point was just not an option ... we had nowhere else to go. And we were learning several strategies that were really working.

Learning a new way

We all do what we think is right for our children. We love them equally but need to treat them uniquely according to their needs. Sam's needs were very different from Izzy's, which is why the behaviour modification approach was required. We were desperate, but, being the eternal optimist that I am, I was always hopeful that there was a solution. I continued researching and exploring. I kept an open mind, I asked for help, I listened to advice. I now believe this was the key that allowed me to problem-solve at last.

I'd thought that parenting didn't need to be taught, that raising and nurturing your children with love was the most instinctive activity in life. How my view has changed! I learned that parenting is a deeply conditioned state that is based on our own experiences of being parented, which may or may not have been positive. But add to this a child with an intense, sensitive, impulsive temperament, and suddenly things become much more complicated. It can feel as if you need to have a degree in child psychology for any chance of being remotely successful.

We were learning how to be effective parents.

We were learning a set of 'core' skills that would help us understand Sam's temperament, make it easier for him to develop his potential, and help us get the best out of family life. Like all parents, we were seeking the holy grail of parenting: keeping calm. And slowly – very slowly, with setbacks aplenty along the way – it was beginning to work.

These were the core skills we were taught:

- *Descriptive praise:* this helped us to develop Sam's motivation, cooperation and confidence. His sense of self-worth started to improve, and as he felt more successful, he became more cooperative. A wonderful positive cycle developed.

- *Reflective listening:* this helped us improve our emotional bond with Sam. When we connected with him, and validated his feelings of anger, hopelessness and frustration, he felt more connected to us and understood, and he became able to manage his emotions more effectively.

- *Preparing for success:* this helped us reduce stressful moments and be less reactive. We started to talk through anything that I knew Sam would find stressful, from exciting trips to New Zealand to the more mundane activities like going to the supermarket.

- *Rules and rewards:* this helped us to formulate, communicate and follow through on rules consistently.

- *Positive discipline:* this helped us understand how to respond constructively to unwanted behaviours, in ways that taught Sam to take responsibility and learn from his mistakes, without making him feel worse or damaging his self-esteem.

We practised our new skills religiously, particularly the descriptive praise. I wouldn't be surprised if others around us thought we'd gone mad as we adopted this alien language: 'Sam, I really appreciate you kept your cool there and just shouted at your sister to show her how mad you were. That was a huge improvement on yesterday when you got angry and hit her. You're learning more self-control – good for you!'

To be honest, I really didn't care what others thought any more. We were seeing results. Our household was becoming more manageable, and we were becoming stronger.

And once we started to see results from the core skills, it allowed us to move on to the next stage in our training, finally working on some 'applied' skills:

- *Fostering independence and encouraging good habits:* we started to apply the core skills to train Sam in the attributes we thought would benefit him as an adult. As well as equipping him with life skills, teaching him to be more self-reliant massively boosted his confidence.

- *Fostering good relationships between siblings:* we began to explore ways to ensure Sam and Izzy had a positive relationship and were able to resolve conflict constructively. All children will bicker and fight; helping them learn dispute resolution is one of the greatest gifts you can give them.

The importance of failure

All of us have failed. Most of us do it regularly. It's the most normal experience in the world, and it's vital we help our children to understand that we can treat failures as learning opportunities. Sam had experienced failure of a spectacular nature at a very young age. He had been to the deepest, darkest place of despair, feeling isolated, lonely and hopeless. After he'd spent eighteen months excluded from normal education, we realised there was nowhere further to fall.

I love J. K. Rowling's motivational speech at the Harvard University commencement in 2008, which illustrates beautifully the power of failure and what the human spirit can reveal in the face of adversity:

Failure gave me an inner security that I had never attained by passing examinations. Failure taught me things about myself that I could have learned no other way. I discovered that I had a strong will, and more discipline than I had suspected; I also found out that I had friends whose value was truly above the price of rubies.

The knowledge that you have emerged wiser and stronger from set-backs means that you are, ever after, secure in your ability to survive. You will never truly know yourself, or the strength of your relation-ships, until both have been tested by adversity. Such knowledge is a true gift, for all that it is painfully won, and it has been worth more than any qualification I ever earned.

As we changed our parenting style and felt more in charge, Sam, in turn, realised he also needed to turn things around and start making his own changes. We were now walking the tightrope between supporting him every step of the way and not 'rescuing' him, allowing him to problem-solve, complete a project himself, and experience that sense of satisfaction.

In doing so, Sam came to realise he wanted to turn his life around.

If you change nothing, nothing will change. Change was needed again.

His own project became getting back into a proper educational environment. Tony and I could not agree more.

Melissa says: The importance of being in charge, not controlling

It's clear that at various points in her story so far, Elaine has felt overwhelmed and let her instincts give way to the advice of professionals. She did need professional support and the help she got generally made a very positive difference to the Halligan family. But she also needed to trust her own instincts to be able to take on those aspects of the advice that worked for her, and modify or ditch the rest. Consider this wise piece of advice from the Buddha: 'Believe nothing, no matter where you read it or who has said it, not even if I have said it, unless it agrees with your own reason and your own common sense.'

When I first met the Halligans I'd been working at the Hawthornes Centre for four-and-a-half years. Sam was attending the centre and I was the facilitator assigned to work with the family at home. I can remember the first time Elaine and Tony came to my home and they told me about Sam and his diagnoses. I hadn't previously worked with anyone diagnosed with PDA. When I was being flippant I described this condition as being characteristic of someone who didn't do as they were told. I'd certainly had experience of that in my work (and at home)! The Halligans had been advised that they should avoid giving Sam any direct instructions. Fortunately, I was ignorant enough and enthusiastic enough about the skills I'd been trained in to ignore that advice! I helped Elaine and Tony require good behaviour of him while connecting with him and addressing the reasons why he misbehaved.

I loved the skills I'd learned at Hawthornes, particularly descriptive praise, reflective listening and the ideas around positive discipline. I embraced the idea of being both positive and firm at the same time, but by now I was having some reservations about the way the concept of firmness was applied. I'd understood that restraints were only to be used in order to avoid a child hurting themselves or someone else or damaging property, not as consequences for misbehaviour. While the director of the centre wanted to ensure the children followed the rules, the rigid and exacting way in which these were enforced was something I became increasingly unhappy with. Near enough was never considered good enough, despite the effort it may have taken children to achieve what had been asked of them. To my way of thinking this was not 'being in charge' but being overcontrolling. When I left to set up The Parent Practice eighteen months later this was one of the distinctions I wanted to make.

Parents do need to be in charge, of course. Because we have greater experience, perspective and a more mature brain which gives us greater powers of reasoning and self-control. But if we are overcontrolling we will create resentment and resistance. As with so many aspects of parenting, it's a question of balance.

Alfie Kohn, in his book *Punished by Rewards*, suggests that parents should always ask themselves the question, are we doing what we're doing in order to help the child or just to get him to obey? He thinks that many people adopt a controlling approach because of a mistaken view that the alternative to control is permissiveness. This is pendulum thinking. I found myself doing this when my older son was behaving badly as a little boy. I would try a positive approach and then conclude that it hadn't worked (as he was misbehaving) and so would come down hard on him with punishment. I'd then feel remorseful and try the softer approach again. Success came when I discovered that I could be positive and firm at the same time.

Parents find themselves on a spectrum between 'controlling or authoritarian' on the one end and 'permissive' on the other. Somewhere in between is the 'authoritative' parent. These parents are in charge but are not overcontrolling. Their rules are about teaching the child, not being 'the boss'. Their steps to control are in order to teach the child self-control. Their methods of discipline are to teach the child self-discipline. The child has input but isn't ruling the roost.

If we overcontrol our children the danger is that we may:

● provoke rebellion, as they feel manipulated and nagged;

● create dependency on us – they don't learn to think for themselves and they don't develop responsibility;

● create docility, as their spirit is broken.

Parenting works best when it is about encouraging, not forcing. If you want to motivate a child to do what they should do, don't make them fear you.

If you want to raise a child to be an adult who can speak up for their own needs, solve problems and sometimes question authority then you will need to allow them to express opinions. If they are to be emotionally intelligent adults they need to learn that their feelings count in childhood. If you want to raise a child who can be creative and solve problems then involve them in problem-solving.

This balancing act can be very hard to get right. It starts by being curious about a child's behaviour. It begins with the assumption that children want to do the right thing and acceptance that they will make mistakes. It continues with the idea that when they get something wrong they deserve to be treated with respect and helped to make amends and learn from the episode.

Elaine and Tony were learning to be in charge through the use of clear and consistent rules. At The Parent Practice we developed the use of rules not as a controlling dogma, but as a proactive parenting tool to enable parents to pass on values to their children. The Halligans combined their rules with much descriptive praise and emotion coaching (explained in the next two chapters).

So what puts us in charge?

- Clear and consistently applied rules that tell the child what to do, not what not to do. Ideally these should be written down or in picture form so that we are not telling our children what to do all the time, leaving them feeling nagged and controlled.

- But rules are a blunt instrument without a relationship. We need to build a positive relationship with our children by spending time with them doing fun things and by the use of positive language.

- Positive language includes descriptive praise but it's also just engaging in conversation (no electronic devices!) and asking kids open-ended questions to find out about their likes and dislikes, interests and passions, fears and worries, and their opinions. Positive language also means avoiding:

    > Nagging (including repeating and reminding): 'I've told you a hundred times to take your feet off the sofa.'

    > Criticising: 'You've forgotten your trumpet again, you silly boy.'

    > Scolding or telling off: 'This is just not good enough, Josh. Your behaviour this week has been deplorable.'

    > Put-downs or name-calling: 'Oh, you are such a baby.'

    > Labelling: 'You're so mean/forgetful/silly/stupid.'

    > Sarcasm: 'Well that's a clever thing to do!'

    > Threatening: 'If you don't behave better at school Charlie won't be coming for a sleepover this weekend.'

    > Humiliation: 'Only an idiot would do something like this.'

> Lecturing or advising: 'If I were you I would go and see your friend and try and explain …'

> Judging or blaming: 'This is so like you, you are always reacting like this.'

> Dismissing or denying their feelings: 'You can't be feeling sad about such a little thing/no, you're not scared/you'll be fine/you don't hate your sister.'

> Comparing: 'Sarah can do it and she's younger than you.'

- Using positive body language, since positive language includes the non-verbal aspects of communication too.

- Discipline that is focused on teaching, not hurting or being 'the boss'.

- Paying attention to, acknowledging and teaching children to manage their feelings. This puts kids in charge of their emotions rather than being driven by them.

- Giving children some control. They may not be able to choose whether or not something is done but they can have some input into the how, when and where of the task. All of us need some control over our own lives to feel happy.

- Above all, parents need to keep calm in order to be in charge. If you lose it you're definitely not in charge and your kids know it. That means looking after ourselves (not just physically, but emotionally as well) and understanding ourselves well. We need to know why certain behaviours push our buttons and make us see red to the point that all our skills fly out the window. I realised that this was a missing piece of the parenting puzzle, so when I formed The Parent Practice I trained with Bonnie Harris and incorporated into our programmes many of the ideas from her book *When Your Kids Push Your Buttons*. Elaine and Tony learned to change their thinking about Sam's behaviour, to check their assumptions and re-examine their beliefs, so that they could adjust their responses when he slipped up and calmly take steps to address whatever was needed.

Elaine's reflections

1. Medication for children is often a last resort for parents. If this has been suggested for your child, what alternatives have you researched?

2. Realising you have an atypical learner often means you have to recalibrate what is normal. Is your child suited to the traditional learning environment or do you believe you, too, may have to recalibrate normality?

3. Parenting is a deeply conditioned state based on one's own experiences of being parented. How has your experience affected how you parent today?

4. Positive parenting skills can help form a solid foundation for connecting with your child. Have you ever tried a parenting course? If not, what has stopped you?

5. Failures should be treated as learning opportunities. Think of a time when your child failed. How did they cope? Did they learn from the experience?

Further reading

Bonnie Harris, *When Your Kids Push Your Buttons: And What You Can Do About It*, 2005.

Alfie Kohn, *Punished by Rewards: The Trouble with Gold Stars, Incentive Plans, A's, Praise and Other Bribes*, 1999.

5

This Changes Everything

(Back to School)

Praising children is not merely a bit of luxury, some additional fancy wrapping that we can leave off if we prefer ... [it] is at least as important as being properly fed and clothed.

Elizabeth Hartley-Brewer,
Raising and Praising Boys

The placement at the Hawthornes Centre came to a natural end after eighteen months as the programme closed. Once again, we had to seek a new school for Sam. But Hawthornes had always been intended as a remedial step, not a long-term solution, and we'd come so far since the last school search that all of us felt Sam needed to return to a more traditional learning environment. 'My ambition is to go to a proper school,' declared Sam proudly, 'and wear a school uniform.'

He was almost nine and had already been in four educational establishments. By this time, I'd seen almost all the specialist provisions in London for children with learning needs. In our desperation to find an answer to help our son, we'd also tried out most of the alternative therapies supported by any shred of evidence. We'd spent a considerable amount of money on a programme that promised to be the miracle cure for dyslexia, only for the company to be shut down after a false advertising dispute. We'd tried coloured glasses for Irlen syndrome to help him track text better when reading. We'd used the brushing technique for sensory integration, applied deep pressure to try and calm his senses, supplemented his diet with omega-3 fatty acids and taken him to several sessions of cranial osteopathy. I was consumed by researching and implementing these therapies. I wasn't going to give in. I was on a mission to ensure our son could lead as normal a life as possible, even though everything at this point was far from normal.

I reflected on this as I thumbed through the pages of the Gabbitas guide, with its listings of hundreds of schools for special needs, looking for one that might take Sam. I realised I must have seemed like an obsessive mother over the past few years. I'd gone to extraordinary lengths to find a 'miracle cure'. There was an abundance of providers out there – so many doing invaluable work (and some that just seemed to exploit vulnerable parents) – I had to investigate them all. Surely one of them would be able to help my son. By this point, I'd actively sought help from fourteen different establishments that I felt had the potential to help, including speech and language centres, specialists in sensory integration, optometrists for coloured glasses, and various dyslexia support centres, not to mention every school that supported children with SEN. Many of these schools were doing outstanding work and were run by committed and devoted educationalists, but they kept turning us away, saying they weren't right for Sam. The pattern that emerged was that they either catered for children with more severe learning needs than Sam's, or they felt his behavioural issues were too great for them to handle. We were stuck between a rock and a hard place. It was such an exhausting, time-consuming process, and again I felt myself sinking into frustration and despair, battling to fend off hopelessness. Surely there were other children like Sam, who had an above-average IQ but nevertheless struggled in education?

Driving on

Later that week, my head still spinning with decisions to make, we had a meeting with our LEA caseworker. She suggested we look at a little school in Surrey called Knowl Hill. 'Another prospectus to be added to the pile, another school to visit,' I thought. And this one was miles away from us. But as I looked through the pages, I started to feel more hopeful. It was a very small, family-run school, established especially for children with dyslexia and associated learning needs, and they took children from the age of seven. We hadn't come across one like it yet.

Knowl Hill School prides itself on being a happy, nurturing environment where our children can flourish and achieve. We also believe that all our pupils have unique gifts and talents. At Knowl Hill we like to capitalise on these strengths, offering a curriculum tailored to their particular gifts, whilst teaching all subjects in a more creative way. We aim to develop lively, inquiring minds and to help pupils acquire the knowledge and skills to either return to mainstream education or gain qualifications matching their capabilities.

It sounded heaven sent. We arranged a visit. They assessed Sam, and offered him a place right away. They wanted him! I could have wept with joy, but held it together so as not to embarrass Sam. The head and deputy were such warm people, and I immediately saw how they both had that rare gift of seeing the good in all their pupils. They truly demonstrated their belief that each child is unique, and with their experience were able to tailor every aspect of the curriculum to accommodate Sam's needs. We knew this was the sign of a really great school that was suited to help Sam and his needs.

Sam's memories of Knowl Hill remain vivid today.

It seemed enormous to me, having come from a place where there'd been only four of us, to a school of sixty boys and girls. It was a proper school, with a little playground, a car park and a brilliant creative block at the back where we did art, woodwork and tech. All relatively normal!

The downside was the journey. From our home in south London all the way to a picturesque village in Surrey, it was a daily commute of seventy minutes each way – not quite your local school every parent hopes for! But Sam's case was not unique; many boroughs lack appropriate schools and have no choice but to place children elsewhere. At this time, our borough was also sending two other boys to Knowl Hill, so the three of them were provided with a taxi service every day. Sam loved it! He always sat in the front, next to the driver, chatting incessantly and reeling off questions. He still remembers all the drivers (and there were many) and their cars in remarkable detail, making for an extensive catalogue of models including:

- a Skoda Fabia Estate;

- a green Ford Mondeo;

- a silver Ford Mondeo – an automatic with a luxury pack;

- a gold Ford Mondeo – very highly spec'd;

- Tony the Tiger's old burgundy London taxi – this jalopy really struggled down the A3;

- a Renault Megane …

And so Sam's love affair with motors, ignited all those years ago by watching Annabel with her camper van, was now fuelled by his daily travels down the A3 and through the Surrey hills in a variety of automobiles. But little did we know just how significant this passion would become.

The mistakes process

Sam's confidence was returning. He loved being in a proper school environment and putting on a school uniform every morning, and despite the gruelling journey there and back every day, he settled in well and made tremendous progress. Hayley was still living with us and would spend all day at school with Sam too. She nurtured a great relationship with him.

Within the first term he'd settled down well in class. The school even reported that when he worked well, his performance was above average within his year group. However, he still needed a lot of support, and had to understand everything fully before he could begin a task. When this wasn't possible, he was quick to show his frustration, and it dented his confidence in his own ability.

He often struggled to find the right words to say. It was evident he had significant language processing issues and difficulty understanding what people were saying to him, so he started having intensive speech and language therapy at school.

Teachers reported he would often be the classroom clown still, doing everything to make the others laugh. We were already familiar with this defence mechanism, and while it hadn't always worked before, in this school he quickly became popular with the other children, and as his confidence increased he stopped feeling the need to play this role.

However, there was one area he still really struggled with, and that was controlling his anger. He often told me he was concerned about losing his temper, and wanted to know what he could do about it. He started to become acutely aware of his impulsivity and lack of self-control and, paradoxically, this seemed to cause him to explode even more often. He would lash out aggressively – hitting, kicking, spitting – yet every time, post-explosion, he would be utterly remorseful. 'I don't know why I do it, why I did it again,' he'd tell me. 'I just couldn't help myself.'

In the spring term of his first year, I received a call from the head to say they'd had to suspend Sam from school for the rest of the week. 'Please, no. Not another exclusion.' There'd been an altercation in the science lab that day. Sam had been working with another little boy and they were struggling to share and cooperate. Sam had snatched something from him, knocking over a Bunsen burner, which had caught a glass vial and the whole lot smashed to the floor. There'd been panic among the children; Sam had got madder at the reaction of those around him and, with that, he'd started to turn over chairs and before he knew what was happening the lab was being evacuated.

When Sam came home that day, I already knew the details of what had happened. He was clearly feeling very sorry for himself, and remorseful.

When our children make mistakes, it's easy to speak to them in a way that suggests we think they're wrong, bad, naughty and wicked. We often speak in a judgemental way. ('What on earth were you thinking? Didn't you realise what the consequences would be? It's such a naughty thing to have done.')

But this time, I used everything I'd learned from Melissa and the Hawthornes Centre to have a calm, positive conversation. 'I know what's happened at school today in the science lab,' I said, as we took a seat at the kitchen table. 'I'm guessing you're probably feeling very upset, perhaps even embarrassed and wishing the whole event just hadn't happened. It may have even been quite frightening for you once you realised what was going on.'

And instead of coming out with excuses or venting his frustration, Sam simply told me what had happened.

I just got so angry, Mum. Charlie wasn't listening to me. He was being silly and unreasonable. But I didn't mean to push him, or knock over the burner or smash the vial. It was an accident. I didn't do it on purpose.

I hugged him tightly.

I'm so glad you didn't do this intentionally. I know you have a moral compass and that you understand the difference between right and wrong. You don't need a lecture from me about that. I also know the school have delivered a consequence, that you are suspended for tomorrow and can return on Monday once things have calmed down. You helped set the lab straight, picking up the chairs and clearing up the glass, didn't you? So you've already made a good start in setting wrong to right. I wonder if there's anything else you can think of to make amends for this?

Together, Sam and I worked through possible solutions and he decided that he would pay for the broken vial using his birthday money. As he did, it dawned on him this was the money he'd been saving to buy one of his prized die-cast cars – the 1:24 model of the Lamborghini Sesto Elemento with its 5.2 litre V10 engine – shattering that dream. Worse still, I suggested he write an apology note to the teacher. He found it so hard to put pen to paper, and I saw on his face how much this stung. But when he eventually agreed he would, something fascinating came out of it. He wasn't apologising for getting angry – this was something he couldn't help; everyone gets angry. Rather, he was apologising for what happened as a consequence of his anger, and that he wasn't able to rein it in before it got out of control. This was the moment it became clear to him that he needed to work out what he could do differently next time he got cross.

As a result of this event, and the apology note, Sam and his teachers invented a coloured card system. He would now carry a red card in his jacket pocket and if he felt he was struggling emotionally at any time at school, all he had to do was show the card to the teacher. No words were required; that was the sign he needed help. If necessary, he could exit the classroom to calm down. This simple strategy worked, and just the presence of the red card seemed to help Sam be more aware of his emotions and thus his behaviour.

This whole process enabled Sam to take responsibility for what happened. Importantly, it allowed him to forgive himself, to accept that making a mistake did not make him a bad person, and to understand that he could make amends for the mistake and learn from it.

I only wish adults were able to use this process more often and take responsibility for their mistakes. It is critically important that we model good behaviour for our children, leading by example. We all make mistakes – it's a completely normal part of life. But what we do with them and how we make amends is where the learning happens.

Hope returns

One of the hardest things for a parent with a child who is different is finding the right educational environment, a school that truly nurtures the child and understands their unique temperament and qualities. Not only did Knowl Hill understand Sam, but they were also willing to tailor both the curriculum and the disciplinary process to his needs. I really felt we had struck lucky.

'But it was a big change for me,' Sam told me recently when we were chatting about the school. 'While I did have Hayley there to look after me, I found it all quite terrifying. I really struggled in the first year and felt unsettled. I still acted out and could get very aggressive.'

Despite this, there was no doubt that Sam's self-control was improving. He interacted well with the other students in the classroom and playground. The staff were positive and encouraging, and very receptive to learning new approaches for managing behaviour in the classroom, which the school was happy to provide. Melissa had been in several times to observe Sam in the classroom and even delivered a training session for the staff. This not only benefited Sam but all the other children as well. Using the right language and good preparation, breaking tasks down into munchable chunks, the teachers started getting through to Sam.

A report from his games teacher at the end of the year read:

Sam showed great self-control when he was paired with another student who was throwing the bean bag to him in such a way that Sam could not catch it. Sam seemed irritated, but retained his good humour.

I read it again:

Sam seemed irritated, but retained his good humour.

To many, this might be unremarkable. But to us, it was a mighty leap forward in Sam's progress.

Aged nine, Sam went on his first school trip. Six days in Italy! It was incredibly ambitious, both for Sam and for the school, but, since the day he learned to let go of me at the nursery gates, Sam had always demonstrated a fiercely independent streak. He heard about the trip and he wanted to go on it, more than anything, so we took the plunge and let him go.

He returned brimming with excitement and grinning from ear to ear. The school's report was largely positive:

Sam coped very well on the trip, given that he was the youngest and had never been on a residential trip before. He had to share the room and facilities with the other children. There was one incident where he kicked and spat at Hayley and another member of staff because he was not getting his own way. He had money held back as a consequence, and he did comment afterwards that he was sad he could not buy something he wanted, so this served as a good lesson. On the plane, he sat by himself and coped very well. We would certainly take Sam away again.

Travel and adventure have continued to feature strongly in Sam's life until today. While he might have inherited a thirst for adventure from me and Tony, I am certain that the residential trips he went on while at Knowl Hill – to Rome, Pompeii and Auschwitz – played a significant role in developing his independence and nurturing his natural curiosity to see more of the world.

Sam agrees: 'This is definitely where I got my travelling bug. The trips were always successful for me as the staff understood me so well.'

For the first time in his life, Sam started to make real friends. He met the McTaggart brothers, Angus and Elliott, and they remain firm friends to this day, sharing his passion for adventure.

When Sam talks about their friendship today, it's clear how significant it was not only for him to have companions, but also in how it helped him understand others.

I met Angus on my first day at Knowl Hill – we were instantly inseparable. He had a calming influence on me. Although neither of us could really read or write, we found success in the design studio, getting our hands dirty and creating things. We recognised a different form of intelligence in each other and had a mutual respect for each other. He's probably the cleverest person I know – not in the sense of being an intellectual, but he can fix a car and put an engine together. He's an incredible artist and has an eye for detail and precision that defies belief. It's really hard to explain – he does everything so precisely – you shouldn't be able to do something so precisely unless you calculate it, but he never calculates anything …

Sam trails off, deep in thought, before adding, 'I guess that's the beauty of dyslexia.'

They had so much fun as kids. Sam spent many weekends on the McTaggarts' farm. He recently told me of the things they got up to, smiling broadly as he recalls them.

We built dens, treehouses, go-karts, and we used to drive his parents' ex-MOD Land Rover. We couldn't even reach the seat. We had to climb into it! I think this was the time I really started to become a petrolhead. Angus was really interested in how things worked – I just wanted to drive.

I'd been blissfully unaware that my eleven-year-old Sam had driven a Land Rover on the farm! He'd known what my reaction would have been – an outright *no!* I certainly would have condemned it as being too dangerous, and I can't even bring myself to think of the accidents that could have happened in such a powerful vehicle. Yet as he tells me this, despite myself, I feel joy for these adventures he had, running free and getting grubby, limited only by his imagination, free from the watch of an overprotective society, free from the binds of any helplessness imposed on him by others. He was starting to make his own path to becoming a competent and capable young man.

I now believe this is the key to progress and success. Finding the right environment at school as well as at home. Enabling children to feel competent and successful in all areas of their life, not just the academic side. We *couldn't* focus on the academic side, as Sam's emotional needs were paramount. If you manage, in any way you can, to find strong, wise men and women who understand your child, and who are willing to take the time to get to know them, then the path to progress will emerge. For us at that time, our strong, wise man was

Mr Dow Grant, the head teacher at Knowl Hill. He was a jovial yet authoritative figure. Recognising each child's strengths was second nature to him. He'd even had wristbands created that said 'You've been caught being good!', and he handed these out to the children to encourage them to focus on their own good behaviour. With his approach, together with all the positive parenting skills we were implementing at home, things started to work out and Sam's behaviour began to transform.

The annual duck race was the highlight of the school year. They put on an incredible summer fete, with stalls and games (and not forgetting the ducks). Every child had a role in the event, which further strengthened their sense of self-worth. They loved it, and everyone involved felt a real sense of community and belonging.

Seeing the transformation in Sam since I'd changed my parenting methods, and watching him thrive, at long last, in such a positive atmosphere at school, made me think about my own role in life. It wasn't hard for me to see (although it was hard to admit) that my career as an accountancy lecturer had fallen flat. But at the same time, I'd learned so much about parenting, psychology and children, and even our interactions with one another in general, that I started to think about retraining as a parenting coach myself.

As this idea grew, I felt a new sense of purpose. In addition to helping my own family, I could help others in the process. Having a sense of purpose is essential for living a fulfilled and happy life, and I deeply believe that opportunity arises from even the most trying challenges. This is how we grow. And so my training as a parenting coach began. I joined The Parent Practice, where I trained with Melissa, and there I remain today. In the midst of trying to help Sam, I had found a new role for myself.

Buoyed

As Sam grew more confident and independent, it became clear that the time was coming for him to separate from Hayley. This coincided with Hayley taking the decision to move back to South Africa. It was sad to see her go, but we all knew the time was right.

Despite his behavioural and social progress, the end of each school year always brought a large, dark cloud over us. Sam's statement of SEN (now known as an education, health and care (EHC) plan) meant our LEA reviewed his progress every year and assessed whether the current school placement remained appropriate. Budgets were always tight and resources had to be allocated to those who needed them most.

We had been having annual reviews for the past six years, and the stress never eased. I slept restlessly the night before every meeting as there was always the risk that the LEA would withdraw funding or ambush us with plans to educate Sam elsewhere.

The meetings were formal, stuffy affairs, and inexplicably held in cramped rooms. There'd often be nine of us sardined together around a table:

- me;
- Tony;
- the head teacher;
- the statement monitoring officer;
- the family and school support manager;
- the occupational therapist;
- the speech and language therapist;
- the classroom teacher; and
- the learning support assistant.

Tony and I would enter the room and be met with a sea of faces, some familiar, some completely new; much time was spent on introductions. Some years, the representing officer wouldn't even have met Sam in person; to them, my son was just a number and a tsunami of paperwork.

They'd look at Sam's progress, hear everyone's views on how he was doing, read a report that Sam had written on how he felt he was doing, and assess whether the school was meeting his needs. The taxi costs to get Sam to school were the most contentious issue with his placement at Knowl Hill, although the school's fees were reasonable compared to other specialist provisions.

After four years at the school, Sam started to get restless. He knew he'd made considerable progress behaviourally and socially; he rarely got into serious trouble these days and was well liked by pupils and staff. But the more time he spent with his friends, the more he became aware that he wasn't progressing at the same pace as them academically. His language processing difficulties were so severe that he hadn't responded to any conventional specialist approaches tried so far. But Tony and I had focused almost entirely on Sam's behaviour for so many years, so it came as a shock when we realised that Sam, aged eleven and a half, had the reading and comprehension skills of a six-year-old.

That year, in his pupil review report, Sam wrote: 'I'm desperate to learn how to read now. I just feel so frustrated. I want to move schools.'

We arrived at the meeting ready to fight our corner for what seemed like the hundredth time. But this time, we recognised everyone. Looking around the room, we realised it was just school staff there. The LEA had failed to send an officer.

The meeting went ahead, and Mr Dow Grant explained that because the LEA was not represented at the meeting, Sam's wishes could not be challenged, and as long as the next school we chose was within budget, they had no option but to agree.

As Sam had got older, the savings the LEA could make on him had become less significant. Other cases that had more chance of being contested successfully had taken priority.

The fight was over. His funding was secure.

So in the spring term of 2008, I found myself immersed in piles of prospectuses, yet again. Over the next three months, I wrote to half a dozen more schools, attaching Sam's statement and asking if they would consider him for a place. From speaking to friends and acquaintances, a firm favourite emerged. More House School, despite being even further from us, in a far corner of Surrey, would be perfect for Sam. It was a centre of excellence in terms of teaching boys with dyslexia. Sam would have access to a full curriculum and benefit from the wide variety of subjects on offer. And, with a roll of around four hundred boys, it really felt like the proper secondary school Sam was after. We all had our hearts set on it.

But for all my efforts, only two schools responded positively, and More House wasn't one of them. Both were boarding schools that Sam really didn't want to go to. I was devastated.

We had a major problem. While Sam's statement of SEN had served us well over the past six years, it was now a handicap, presenting an out-of-control child who had extreme anger management issues. Most schools wouldn't touch him with a bargepole!

His mood swings can be sudden and quite extreme and this is likely to be attributable to anxiety and pathological demand avoidance. He is resistant to adult direction and has difficulty managing his behaviour. He has Asperger's syndrome and sensory integration disorder.

Nowhere in the statement did it mention how he'd progressed behaviourally and socially, or that his latest educational psychology report no longer focused on his behaviour but the severity of his dyslexia and language processing difficulties. And not only was Sam labelled on his statement, but his reputation among the local schools was also tarnished.

We, and everyone who knew Sam, recognised that the Asperger's diagnosis was simply incorrect, and that the PDA was a state induced by extreme anxiety and frustration. We had clear evidence that with the right support at home and at school, Sam could manage his behaviour. We knew that underneath all his issues, which were being carefully addressed, a diamond was beginning to glisten. And with every challenge we faced, I became ever more determined to reveal it.

I knew what I needed to do. I had to get the current statement rewritten. For this, I needed a good dose of luck on my side. My father's words rang in my ears: *you create your own luck.* I called him for a pep talk. 'You need to be optimistic, Elaine, you know this!' he said, ever positive, ever supportive. 'Stay on the lookout for opportunities. Trust your gut instinct. Transform bad luck into good. Now go and arrange that meeting – if anyone can do it, you can!'

Two weeks later, just days before the schools broke up for the summer holidays in early July 2008, I went to the LEA with an air of optimism and positive expectation. And I lucked out. I landed myself a senior caseworker who'd been brought out of retirement to cover for a colleague. He had been there and done it all. He had years of wisdom and experience, and when I explained my situation, all he said was, 'Mrs Halligan, let's get this statement rewritten. Tell me what you think it should say.'

Within two hours, the statement was turned around. Now it focused on Sam's progress, described the environment he needed in order to nurture his skills in managing his own behaviour, and detailed his specific learning needs. This gave Sam a modicum of hope to try for the change of placement he wanted.

Armed with our new statement and my rehearsed explanations that there had been some remarkable improvements, I went back to More House. I kept thinking as positively as I could, stamping down the doubts that reared their ugly heads, 'Will they recognise the application as one they previously rejected? Will they give us a chance?'

Someone, somewhere, surely had to believe in this little boy.

Melissa says: The importance of descriptive praise in raising self-esteem

It's easy to underestimate the impact of our words on our children. Two of the skills Elaine and Tony used with Sam that really helped to turn his life around were descriptive praise and emotion coaching. These two skills, incredibly powerful in combination, allow our children to feel seen and heard.

Most parents try to praise their children, although many regret they don't do it enough. It's relatively easy to praise a child when they're behaving well (and when we're well rested and on the ball) but the praise I learned about was different. When I first heard about descriptive praise I thought it sounded a really good idea ... in theory. I thought it would work really well on *other* children ... 'good' ones. But not on my son. To begin with I found it very difficult to find anything praiseworthy about his behaviour.

Like Sam, my older boy is bright, and dyslexic. He found the gap between what was going on in his head and what he could produce in the classroom confusing and frustrating. He was convinced he was stupid. Like Sam, he used many strategies to avoid doing the work that was so hard for him and so was disruptive. Like Sam, his frustration sometimes erupted in aggressive behaviour. He got in trouble a lot and believed he was bad.

Just like Elaine and Tony did with Sam, we needed to change my son's view of himself. Slowly, but surely, through lots of observations of others, I learned to look for very small examples of good behaviours and mention them to him. I sometimes found it difficult when he was in front of me, provoking me. I'd got into the habit of expecting poor behaviour and that was what I noticed first. In our classes we do an exercise that reveals how common this approach is. We are conditioned to notice what is wrong with something and we mention it to our children in the hope of getting the behaviour to change. Our intention is not to hurt, but to teach.

My strategy was to sit down when my son was at school and write down some positive things I could say to him. I was surprised with how many I found. I'd intended to keep this piece of paper handy to pull out when I was stuck. The first time I went to use it my son asked me what it was and I explained it was a list of good things I'd noticed about him. He was amazed. 'You mean you were thinking about me when I was at school and you wrote all that down?' He didn't think there'd be that many good things to record either. That was heart-wrenching and made me resolve to look more carefully for the positives.

We get more of the behaviours we pay attention to. Unfortunately most of us don't notice when our children are sitting quietly at the dinner table, using their cutlery, trying their food and being nice to their siblings. We just get on with our lives – maybe with our eyes on our mobile devices. But we jump on the behaviour when they start flicking peas across the room. Our children find it easier to get the attention they crave for negative behaviours.

When parents do praise their children they generally use phrases like 'well done', 'good boy', 'clever girl', 'that's awesome', 'you're brilliant' or 'you're an amazing artist/footballer'.

When we ask parents why they praise their kids they say they want to:

1. reinforce a particular behaviour;

2. build a positive relationship with their child; and

3. encourage self-esteem.

Conventional praise is not bad at the second of these objectives but is pretty useless at items 1 and 3. Why? Standard praise isn't specific enough for a child to be able to reproduce the behaviour or for it to have much credibility. It tends to be evaluative and sometimes a bit over the top. It's easy to toss a 'good boy/girl' over your shoulder without paying that much attention, and your child doesn't get the information that would help them focus on the small steps in the right direction. They don't believe you when you say they're the best – especially if they've just got in trouble for speaking rudely to a teacher. They think it's your job as a parent to say that sort of thing.

Ask yourself how it feels if I say: 'You're an amazing mum/dad.' But what if I say: 'You are going to such trouble to really find out what makes your son tick. You've researched his condition, you've been to see specialists and you're here today to find out more behavioural strategies. I want to acknowledge your commitment to him.' The detail is what makes it meaningful. It obviously takes more effort but it is much more effective.

So descriptive praise is specific. It focuses on the small steps in the right direction.

We use descriptive praise to motivate and to build strong self-esteem. But if you wait for something significant to happen you lose the motivating effect of the praise. When my older boy was in primary school they had a system of merits and demerits to acknowledge good and bad behaviour respectively. A teacher explained to me that you could only get a merit for quite significant behaviour. But demerits were given out very freely! My younger son went to a different school and he was awarded a house point on his very first day for 'settling in well at his new school'. It may not have been that descriptive but my boy was hooked!

The first time Sam came with Elaine, Tony and Izzy for a family session at my home we played a card game in my living room. The idea was to observe how the parents interacted with the children and for me to demonstrate the skills that they were learning to use. We have a painting of ships in that room and Sam made some very detailed observations about it. I immediately commented on his perceptive remarks and how politely he'd expressed himself. I observed that that kind of attention to detail would be very useful to him in life. We played UNO (the card game that involves matching colours and numbers) and I descriptively praised both the children (and occasionally the parents) throughout the game for keeping to the rules, for not making a fuss if they got a card that went against them, for taking turns well, for staying at the table and for any other small acts of cooperation. Sam smiled and sat up a bit taller. Despite all the frightening-sounding acronyms that had been applied to him I thought, 'You're no different from anyone else: you want to be good and to get things right, you want to feel good about yourself.'

Descriptive praise allows adults to paint a picture for their children of who they are. Sometimes they have to paint over an old canvas which doesn't show them in a positive light. Sometimes our words have been critical and negative and we have painted a picture of a person who is stubborn or defiant or stupid or selfish or mean or aggressive. If kids think that's who they are then they will behave in ways that fit that model. If they don't think they are worthwhile then they are unlikely to behave in ways that a more valuable person would. That self-fulfilling prophecy is called the Golem effect.

We know how important self-esteem is. It's not about thinking one is perfect or better than others. It's not about being oblivious to our shortcomings. But it is believing that we are of value, that we are lovable and capable.

Someone with healthy self-esteem knows that when they make a mistake it is part of the human condition; they can clean it up, make amends and learn from it. Children with low self-esteem can be hypersensitive to disapproval. They may have difficulties hearing compliments or see criticism where it is not intended, or be so sensitive that they are unable to profit from feedback.

When children have a good sense of self-worth they are more likely to:

- behave well;
- take responsibility for their own actions;
- believe positive feedback and accept negative feedback as a useful contribution;
- try new things and work hard at them;
- try again when things don't work;
- treat others with respect;
- expect to be treated with respect; and
- have positive relationships.

Furthermore, they are less likely to:

- be vulnerable to peer pressure and bullying;
- use substitutes for confidence such as alcohol, drugs and cigarettes;

- engage in unhealthy relationships, sexual or otherwise; and

- need to prove themselves through bragging, lying, putting others down, excessive competition or endlessly pursuing grades, results or qualifications.

Descriptive praise works to build self-esteem because it is specific and credible. Evidence-based praise allows children to develop internal validation rather than relying on the evaluation of someone else. Descriptive praise also focuses more on a child's efforts, and attitudes and strategies employed, rather than results attained. This is particularly important for those kids who don't do well academically or in sport or the arts. It also encourages a growth mindset. We'll go into this more in Chapter 7.

Descriptive praise is one of the most powerful tools in a parent's toolbox and it transformed Sam's self-definition.

Elaine's reflections

1. Alternative therapies such as cranial osteopathy or dietary intervention can have a huge impact on learning and behaviour. Is there a therapy or nutritional supplement you have tried with your child that made a marked difference in their behaviour?

2. Praising your child descriptively can greatly improve cooperation and self-esteem, yet many parents and teachers use conventional, evaluative praise with their children ('good girl', 'well done', 'I'm so proud of you'). Which form of praise are you using?

3. School residential trips can be very valuable to help both parent and child separate and develop the child's independence and self-reliance. Has your child been on their first residential trip yet, and if so, how did you both cope?

4. The mistakes process teaches children how to take responsibility for their mistakes and delivers meaningful, relevant consequences designed to ensure the mistake is less likely to happen again. When your child makes a mistake, do you know how to get them to clear up their mistake and ensure they have strategies to do things differently next time?

5. Sam had a statement of SEN (currently called an EHC plan) that outlined the support he needed, and it helped him access specialist provision. Have you got an EHC plan, and if not, have you come up against resistance in getting one? What strategies have you considered to ensure your child's educational needs are understood?

Further reading

Adele Faber and Elaine Mazlish, *How to Talk so Kids Will Listen and Listen so Kids Will Talk*, 2013.

Elizabeth Hartley-Brewer, *Raising and Praising Boys*, 2005.

6

Revealing the Diamond

(Secondary School)

The ability of a human being to manage his emotions in a healthy way will determine the quality of his life – maybe even more fundamentally than his IQ.

Laura Markham, *Peaceful Parent, Happy Kids*

Transitioning to secondary school is not easy for any child, and many parents will experience anxiety in trying to find the right educational environment. Whether your child is sitting entrance exams or trying to get into the oversubscribed local school, the angst and stress can be overwhelming for everyone.

After all my worries about approaching More House for the second time, I don't think the head even recalled reading the previous version of the statement. That autumn, More House offered us a day for Sam to visit. I was thrilled.

Sam remembers the visit:

It went really well. I was sweating so much with nervous energy that my trousers were sticking to me when I arrived. I was completely overwhelmed by the size of the school. I spent some time doing tests in the learning support department, and I think I was so anxious that I had no capacity to do anything silly! The best thing was that Angus and Elliott McTaggart were also planning to do a trial day. The thought of moving school with my best mates was just brilliant.

All three boys were offered a place starting in January. And the LEA agreed to arrange transport. It was the best

Christmas present ever, and a wonderful, positive, optimistic start to 2009.

Escaping and evading

The first term was traumatic for us all.

I was concerned about another lengthy commute (although for Sam this was the highlight of his day, spending yet more time in cars), but Sam also struggled to settle.

Three days after he'd started at More House, I got a phone call to say he'd gone AWOL and been found walking the back roads of Surrey, trying to get away from school. Apparently he'd just taken his bag, marched off-site and was planning on walking home – over thirty miles away. Sam explains:

I'd planned to get to a local train station and just get myself home. I felt so anxious. I didn't want to be there. I felt a sort of regret, like I'd made the wrong choice, and wanted to go back to Knowl Hill. I'd gone from a tiny school of about fifty pupils to one that seemed enormous, so it was worlds apart from what I knew. The massive variety of ages and friendship groups in the playground was so overwhelming. I saw one of the younger kids get put in a big rubbish bin by the older students. It scared me. It was like nothing I'd experienced before.

Tony picked him up that day to take him home. Sam recalls, 'I was so relieved when Dad came. I cried all over his raincoat and made a bit of a mess.'

Once again, I was beside myself with worry. I immediately phoned Knowl Hill. 'Hi, Mr Dow Grant? It's Elaine Halli— Yes. Hello. Sorry to disturb – we've made the biggest mistake,' I spluttered. 'Would you – do you think – I'm so sorry … could you take Sam back?' I wasn't thinking rationally. My world had collapsed yet again. How many schools could Sam, and we, endure? Life seemed so completely unfair. In that moment, I found myself thinking, 'Why can't I just have a normal child, at a normal school, like everyone else?' I wanted to be in Italy, not Holland. *I hate Holland!*

'Of course Sam can come back, at any time,' replied Mr Dow Grant. 'But don't forget that Sam doesn't cope with change easily, so it might be best for you to hang in there and see this through.'

We took his advice. More House were happy to keep working with Sam, although he was put on close watch, and for the next couple of weeks my life was on hold again as I had to stay near the school all day, from drop-off to pickup, in case something else happened. I got to know the municipal swimming pool and local coffee shops better than those in our own neighbourhood, setting up my mobile office anywhere I could find for a few hours at a time.

Sam's major issue was definitely a lack of impulse control. Despite great improvements, he was still quick to anger, and rarely could anyone see or predict the trigger. A couple of days after 'the great escape', his form tutor, Mrs Stiff, wrote his name up on the board for a minor misbehaviour, and Sam saw red. It brought back those days in primary school when he was labelled a naughty, stupid little boy. He couldn't cope with this public humiliation (as he saw it) and bolted out of the classroom, locking himself in the staff toilet.

Mrs Stiff still had a class to teach, so she called on the deputy head, Mr Williamson, for help. He really understood Sam and was good at getting the right results out of him. He knew right away that punishing, reprimanding and humiliating him wasn't going to work. So, without lecturing or criticising, he stood outside the toilet and gently chatted to Sam to calm him down. None of the staff could use their facilities that morning; those that tried were met with the sight of the deputy head talking to a toilet door.

After thirty minutes, Mr Williamson calmly said, 'Congratulations, Sam. You've just completed your first detention. We'll see you when you're ready,' and walked off. Five minutes later, Sam opened the door.

This strategy of helping Sam calm down, and then removing the attention he wanted, worked brilliantly to get him back on track, and is a great example of how good the school were at differentiating the discipline system to suit the child. It was inspired, and it worked. Sam still got himself into trouble at times, but the teachers were becoming experts in managing him.

Clarity

Within the first half-term, Sam had been given several detentions, yet somehow always managed to talk his way out of them. I could never comprehend how he did this – he just seemed able to convince people of the injustice of it all. He also had a great respect for the head teacher, Barry Huggett, OBE, who was very supportive and had no intention of giving up on Sam so early on. Sam recalls:

Mr Huggett is an amazing guy, an omnipresence, yet very quiet and introverted. He could say a thousand words with just one look. In fact he rarely talked to anyone one-to-one except in his office. He's a man of structure, driven and determined. It was always clear he devoted his life to education and cared deeply about us and our futures. He made sure every one of us got an education, regardless of our difficulties. He is a very cool guy.

Sam came home angry one evening, having been given a caution. He had been found peeling paint off the old desks in the science room. Marching through the door and throwing his bag on the floor, he muttered, 'I confessed to it when the teacher asked me about it. I didn't say sorry though, because the paint was peeling, so I couldn't help but pick at it.' I saw his point. 'I told the teacher how unsuitable the desks are.'

'How do you mean?' I asked.

'They were designed for practical science work, not for sitting and doing written work. They've been modified poorly, painted badly, they're not suitable for anyone over five feet tall, especially those of us with sensory and spatial awareness issues.' He was right: ergonomically, they were a disaster waiting to happen. 'How can we be expected to concentrate properly when we're forced to sit in such a restricted position? I didn't mean to pick the paint off, I didn't mean to damage the desk. I didn't even realise I was doing it! Anyway, I tried to explain all this to the teacher but she wasn't listening. So I swore at her.'

Swearing aside, this was such a clear and reasoned argument that I confess I was a little impressed. It was my first real glimpse into how Sam's mind worked, and the logic and rational thinking that has now become his signature trait. He then coherently explained that being put on detention would be a waste of time as he wouldn't learn anything from it, so he proposed two things: first, he would apologise to his teacher for swearing; and second, he would organise a time to sand down and repaint the peeling desk as a way of making amends.

I wanted to jump for joy. Faced with a punishment, this boy was able to admit to his mistake, apologise and look for a meaningful, relevant way to put things right. His suggestion would be so much more productive than sitting in a room on detention for half an hour after school. I was so proud. If he could cope this well with things going wrong at the tender age of twelve, he would be unstoppable when he grows up.

The library

In that first year at More House, Sam learned a great deal – not all of it on the curriculum, and some quite unexpected.

He spent a lot of time in the library to escape the stresses of the classroom. One day in there, something happened that all parents dread. We know it's coming but we don't know when, and we just hope our children are able to talk about it when it does. We know that even if they don't look for it, *it* will find them. I'm talking about sex.

We'd tried our best in our household to normalise the idea of sex as nothing naughty or dirty but rather as a healthy activity that we, and all mammals, engage in from young adulthood or whenever the time is right. Sam had already had his sex education lessons at school, we'd read educational books about it together, and both our children had even viewed a mating between our working cocker spaniel and a stud, to demystify the concept and understand it as a natural process. Like most tweens, Sam wasn't remotely interested in sexual activity at this age.

He came home one day, and instead of coming into the kitchen to grab a snack, ask what's for tea and chat to me about his day, he went straight upstairs. I found him curled up in the foetal position on our bed. This set my antennae twitching; something had happened to have made him seek solace and comfort.

'Sam?' I said gently, perching next to him on the bed. 'I have no idea what happened at school today, but I am guessing by the way you are curled up there on my bed, something has really upset you. You may be feeling scared, embarrassed or uncomfortable.'

It didn't seem that long ago when I might have questioned or judged, accused him of doing something wrong or simply demanded he got up and *stopped behaving like this*. But this time, I made it as easy as I could for him to speak to me and open up.

'Mum, it was horrible,' he began. 'I was in the library today, having cool-down time, and some of the sixth formers saw me there. They came up to me, and one of them …' – he paused and looked away from me, before continuing in a quieter voice:

---

he showed me something on his phone. The other lads were all crowding round me looking at the phone, and one of them asked,

'How'd you get that, mate?' to which another replied, 'I just asked her to open up her legs!' They were all laughing about it. It was so disturbing. I just can't get the image out of my head. It was so shocking, Mum – I keep thinking, 'What if that had been Izzy?'

I was so thankful he felt comfortable to tell me. All the emotion coaching I'd been doing with him was working. He knew I'd listen to how he felt, and we could problem-solve together. We ended up talking at length, the conversation materialising into an in-depth discussion about girls, porn, self-esteem, how easy it is for girls to become eager to do things to please others, and how important it was that both he and Izzy knew their own self-worth so they would be less likely to engage in activities unwillingly, and be able to think and act for themselves. Sam went to the library less after that, but thank goodness I finally understood how to listen without judgement, and could help him process this cacophony of feelings.

Horror stories

During the summer term, one of the pupils decided to target Sam as his victim. A very creative and imaginative little boy, he'd clearly been watching too much *Buffy the Vampire Slayer* and *The Vampire Diaries*. He took to threatening Sam daily, saying that he was going to suck his blood. But Sam concluded the boy was just 'weird', and wasn't overly perturbed. He was learning to accept other people's differences. This was a valuable skill to learn at a young age. Maybe the fact that he was different himself helped this awareness.

Just as the summer term was ending, another student began victimising Sam and hacked into his email account. The whole year group started to receive unpleasant emails – apparently from Sam, who was the last to know. The same boy also left unsettling graffiti all over the school toilets, with Sam's name everywhere. Sam told me recently.

The boy was a silent, aggressive type. Me, being an outgoing sort of guy, I'd always try to be friendly and make conversation with him. I think that frightened him or something, so I became his target. He decided to send disturbing emails in my name, but in true dyslexic fashion, I hadn't bothered to read any of them! Then the Nazi graffiti showed up, and horrible messages about the Columbine massacre, all with my name on them. It was a little scary, but the school took it seriously and there was never any inference or questioning that I may have been the culprit.

The funny thing was that everyone knew that the boy had chosen the wrong victim – Sam could never have written graffiti with such elaborate vocabulary and perfect spelling!

Sam grew up quickly that year.

Glistening

In Sam's end-of-year report, in the summer of 2009, Mrs Stiff commented:

Despite his difficult start to the year, Sam has made huge progress, particularly over the last few weeks. He is now beginning to settle in to the school community and is showing a new confidence. He still struggles to identify positive elements of his day, but is beginning to respond well to our system of rewards and consequences. He is still quick to criticise the behaviour and mannerisms of others, whilst remaining sensitive to any comment upon or discussion of his own behaviour. His outbursts are becoming increasingly rare and he is able to maintain mature and thoughtful conversations with an adult in a one-to-one or small group setting. He must be careful to choose his words so that he does not sound rude or overly familiar when speaking to adults. Overall, I am pleased to see him settling in and hope he continues to gain confidence as we move forward to Year 9.

Sam's educational path to date had been haphazard, to say the least. But his teachers liked him enormously. They trusted him and wanted to help. It was such a relief – at long last, we had found Sam's educational home. In a school that offered such a huge array of subjects – from photography and pottery to product design and engineering – and where the children were encouraged to explore and learn, to try, fail, and try again, it was inevitable that every boy there would eventually find his strong suit.

For Sam and Angus, their strong suits were the technical and creative subjects: art, pottery and product design. Here, they truly excelled, and Sam started to challenge and push himself in these areas. He created some amazing pieces, including some Japanese-style pottery and decorating a side panel of an old Jaguar car in a stunningly colourful Moorish design. (This piece was even reported in the local press.)

'I loved 3D and art and getting my hands dirty throwing clay and making pottery,' he tells me. 'I got on really well with my teacher – she just let me use my imagination and creativity without limits.' Sam and Angus both had work submitted to the GCSE Surrey Art Prize, to be awarded by the University for the Creative Arts nearby. They won first and second prize! 'We were amazed. That was a great night, collecting our awards at the ceremony in the university. The only prize I'd won before was "most improved pupil", back in lower school – but never a specific prize for something I was good at!'

He had begun to experience success for the first time in his life – and with this, he flourished.

I felt like I could breathe again.

We'd honestly never imagined Sam would be able to sit any GCSEs. Even by the age of fifteen, his dyslexia showed no signs of improvement. His spelling was very weak. He could write words accurately if they had regular spelling patterns because his phonological processing skills were actually quite good, but even the most common irregular spellings caused him difficulty. In reading comprehension tests, he could read well enough to gain some meaning, but as the texts got more complex he became unable to read with sufficient accuracy to gather more than the bare outline.

He took a Wechsler Individual Achievement Test (WIAT) assessment to evaluate his overall academic progress, and the literacy scores were dismal:

	Standard score	Percentile	Age equivalent
Reading comprehension	69	2	9.08
Word reading	62	1	7.08
Spelling	64	1	7.04

What these scores meant was that, for every hundred children, Sam's word-reading and spelling was worse than everyone else's; and for reading comprehension, he was in the bottom two. On paper, with scores like this, he should never have been able to sit GCSEs. (Indeed, twenty or thirty years ago, he would have been labelled thick, and his education written off entirely.)

Yet here we were, discussing which GCSEs to choose.

He had a high level of intellectual ability – the same 'spiky' profile that was apparent at every assessment he'd ever taken. And he *wanted* to study. He now had an incredibly positive attitude to learning, which I believe came from the strong sense of self-worth that had been nurtured in him over the past few years. He valued his own strengths, and there were many.

I think hidden disabilities, like dyslexia, are some of the cruellest. If undiagnosed and unsupported, dyslexia can be hugely damaging, not only through childhood but also in adulthood, affecting every aspect of life, from daily activities, careers and relationships to self-worth and mental health. Sam had a terrific amount of assistance, without which he would not have managed. Because his reading and handwriting remained a struggle, as did generating ideas for an essay, he received a huge concession for his exams: 25 per cent extra time, plus someone to read him the questions and a scribe to write down what Sam dictated. And he still had speech and language intervention, occupational therapy, and a huge amount of practical support from us – he asked us to help him digest the syllabus by reading everything out loud to him! By the time he was ready to take his exams, I was convinced I could've sat some of them with him and passed!

And so with maths, triple sciences, English speaking and English language, he decided to take 3D art, product design and business communication systems.

For many, the teenage years are the most difficult. But for me, it was the first time in Sam's life that I believed things were going to work out.

'It was such a rich learning environment,' he says of his time at More House. 'Something sort of clicked for me. By Year 10 I was determined to make something of myself and prove lots of people wrong..'

As his mother, I now felt much more in charge, and by this time I'd become heavily involved in managing The Parent Practice. I was walking the talk in my family life and teaching others positive parenting skills.

Sam knew I would always listen to him and validate his feelings. He valued his strengths, and because his self-esteem was now strong, he was able to acknowledge his severe literacy difficulty. He began to realise his dyslexia was actually a strength, as it enabled him to be creative and think outside the box, and he started to wear this badge with pride.

The diamond in the rough was revealed.

Dandelion clock

Izzy had always been our dandelion – bright, resilient and able to flourish anywhere. Sam was our orchid, who would wilt if he wasn't looked after correctly but, under the right conditions and with close care and attention, would bloom spectacularly. The developmental psychologists Bruce J. Ellis and W. Thomas Boyce borrowed these floral terms from a Swedish metaphor, and they can apply to all of us.

Yet as Sam started to bloom, Izzy began to fade. Siblings of children with SEN can often suffer later in life, having experienced social and emotional isolation, and having had to cope with difficult situations on their own for much of their childhood. Izzy, now fourteen, was worried about Sam's future, concerned how he would ever function in adult life. At the same time, she must have felt deserted, with Tony spending much of his working life abroad, and me spending much of my time supporting Sam.

It was then that I realised we'd been neglecting her needs. It had always been clear that she and Sam needed different levels of attention, but we'd focused so much on Sam during Izzy's formative years that she'd begun to perceive herself as less important than Sam. From that moment, I took it upon myself to ensure I spent some quality time with her every day. We baked, we played golf together, we even played Monopoly – Sam and Izzy's favourite game, and the bane of my life. The worst thing about the game is how family love and compassion disintegrate in an instant, replaced by cold, hard, scheming property acumen. (How ironic, indeed, that today both my children want to pursue careers in property!)

Although Izzy loved this extra attention, she was also in the throes of her teens. For a variety of reasons, she'd started to think more deeply about life both at home and at school. The extra time I'd spent connecting with her helped her to open up to me, and she confessed she was feeling a little depressed and no longer believed she was thriving at school.

The impact of being Sam's sister was that Izzy had become very independent in both thought and action, and while we had always encouraged her in this, it did come as a surprise to me when she announced at the start of the new year that she wanted to move schools. She spoke eloquently of feeling that the all-girl school environment was not a healthy one, with many, in her opinion, being overly occupied with how they look.

'Izzy, darling, you're just about to enter into your GCSE year,' I reasoned one evening when I was snuggling her into bed. 'Just hang on in there and we'll look at a move in sixth form.'

But she had the confidence and emotional intelligence to keep talking to me, and when she finally said, with tears in her eyes, 'I feel like my personality is … dropping,' I knew a drastic decision was needed.

I've thought a lot about the impact Sam's behaviour (and our focus on it) has had on his sister. She'd simply had to grow up way too fast. We allowed her to look at some mixed day schools and boarding schools, and after giving it considerable thought over a few weeks, she finally chose my old school – all the way up in Edinburgh (or the Baltic North, as Izzy liked to call it). She felt she needed that change. She'd get some fresh air and have some fun. I was devastated at the thought of our daughter at boarding school, and so far away while Sam, Tony and I were still in London, but I knew it made sense. My parents were up there, after all, and we holidayed several times a year in 'Costa del Fife'. Importantly, the distance from us meant she would have the space to find herself, reinvent herself, as opposed to being 'little sis' to Sam, her dyslexic brother.

Melissa says: The importance of emotion coaching

Sam had trouble managing his feelings. In fact, his feelings were managing him. He would experience anxiety or frustration or anger and would act on those feelings immediately and impulsively, without rational thought. When our children are young this is normal. Our emotions arise in the more primitive parts of the brain: the brainstem and the limbic system. They are regulated by the prefrontal cortex, the part of the brain that deals with rationality, where our executive functions reside. This is the part of the brain that tells you walking out of the school would be a bad idea, or gives you other options for managing your feelings. It's the bit that says 'whoa!' when your impulses tell you to jump off a tall rock into the inviting sea below. It considers whether it's deep enough or if there are rocks. It's the bit that stops you sending terse emails or messages on social media when you're tired late at night.

If your prefrontal cortex doesn't seem that mature, maybe your brain didn't get as much nurturing as it could have when you were a toddler!

When we are young, our rational brains are immature. It takes many years for them to fully develop and it depends on parental input as well. For the rational brain to be able to control the emotional brain there need to be good neural connections between the different parts. This is helped by nurturing parenting.

Children who experience stress in early life, like Sam did, can be left with elevated stress responses which make them overreact to things. Their rational brains have a harder time controlling their emotions. Stress can also have a negative impact on learning as the prefrontal cortex deals with memory and reasoning. And some kids, like Sam, are just more impulsive and highly sensitive by nature and need greater support to calm their impulses.

Luckily, parents can help.

Parents can coach their children in developing emotional intelligence. This allows them to control their impulses and therefore manage behaviour. Emotional intelligence affects a child's health, wealth, happiness, relationship satisfaction and ability to bounce back from adversity. It is widely accepted among researchers and educators today that a person's emotional intelligence is at least as important in his success as his cognitive abilities and, in fact, will impact on his cognitive abilities.

Emotional intelligence is the ability to recognise, regulate and express emotions. It includes empathy, recognising and caring about what others feel, and resilience, the ability to recover from setbacks and try again. Resilience depends on good emotional regulation and the belief in one's own capacity to make changes – e.g. 'I didn't get it right that time but I will next time.' This is clearly linked to self-belief and a growth mindset. (See Chapter 7.)

In a seminar to the leaders of a global manufacturing company with a strong engineering base, Daniel Goleman, the author of *Emotional Intelligence* and a science journalist specialising in behavioural science and the brain, put forward a strong business and scientific case for emotional intelligence as the active ingredient in strong leadership. Writing about it in the *Harvard Business Review*, Goleman said: 'When it comes to the top echelon leaders, companies find that 80–90% of the competencies that distinguish star leaders are built on emotional intelligence.'

Emotional intelligence can be taught. Parents encourage emotional intelligence in their children by being emotion coaches (a term coined by Dr John Gottman, Professor Emeritus of Psychology at the University of Washington and author of *Raising an Emotionally Intelligent Child*).

Emotion coaching involves:

- recognising, respecting and reflecting back to the child what they are feeling (naming the emotion);

- coaching them in how to manage their feelings; and

- modelling expressing and constructively handling our own feelings and respecting others' feelings.

Elaine and Tony became expert emotion coaches and Sam now has a high level of emotional intelligence. You can be an emotion coach too. Here's how to do it:

- Make time to *pay attention* to your child. Stop what you are doing and convey with your body language that you are paying attention. Put aside digital devices!

- *Stay calm and be curious.* Look for the feeling behind your child's action or words and imagine how your child is feeling. *Don't judge.*

- *Reflect it back to them in words.*

  > 'I'm guessing you're feeling really frustrated because your fists are clenched and your shoulders are hunched up around your ears.'

  > 'I know you're nervous. Does your tummy have butterflies in it?'

  > 'Sometimes when you feel really overwhelmed it just all comes out in a rush and that's when you hit.'

  > 'It takes courage to try something if you're worried you might not get it right. I think sometimes you think you might look silly if you make a mistake.'

  > 'For you to shout at me like that, you must have been feeling really upset. I think you felt really let down when I said I couldn't take you swimming after all. Maybe it feels like I didn't care what you wanted.'

  > 'Maybe it feels like people are telling you what to do all day long and you wish you could be the one to say what happens.'

  > 'You wish you didn't have to go to bed. You'd like to be able to stay up as late as Mummy ... Mummy would like to go to bed now too!'

  > 'You must have been feeling really overwhelmed when you walked out of the classroom. Maybe what you had to do felt impossible and you were embarrassed. When you

feel stupid or ashamed you just want to get out of there to stop those horrible feelings!'

It's *not* our job to take away the feelings of upset our children experience. It *is* our job to help them cope with those feelings. Describing the feelings to your child will not 'encourage' the feeling or 'put ideas in their heads'. You know your child. You know this is likely to be what they were feeling. You want to let them know you get it, you know how that feels, you understand and empathise. If you get it wrong you will not create that feeling in your child. But if you get it right they will feel understood and accepted and it will free them up to think more rationally.

- Don't add '*but* this behaviour is unacceptable' or 'but you have to do ...' This negates your previous empathy.

- Once the child's feelings have been heard they are then able to come to solutions, sometimes with help from an adult. *Brainstorm* with children for solutions to problems – don't just tell them what to do. This fosters creative thinking and problem-solving abilities.

When adults describe emotions, connections are made between the child's prefrontal cortex and their limbic system, which forms neural pathways. When a child is consumed with an emotion there is no point in speaking logically to them. You have to speak 'limbic'! Describing their feelings helps them get the feelings under control and to access their rational brain to look for solutions.

For example, eight-year-old Jake, a very sensitive and impulsive boy, was upset about losing a football game and his self-esteem was very low, so he looked for someone else to blame. He felt too vulnerable and not quite secure or capable enough to be able to accept part of the responsibility for the loss. He'd recently moved to the US and things weren't going well in his new school. So he blamed the other team members, calling them 'babies'. His dad and his coach wanted to teach him to respond more sympathetically, but they couldn't get there via his logical brain, which was shut down in that moment. They did try to reason with him at first and were met with stubbornness and rudeness. Instead, they needed to sympathise about the loss, acknowledge how he likes to win, that it feels important to him. He needed some tangible wins to feel good about himself. Only when his feelings were 'out' could the adults help him to see that it is hurtful to call others 'babies' and help him to analyse what went well with the game and where his team needed to improve.

Izzy had also been encouraged to express her feelings, so she knew her parents would listen without judgment or defensiveness when she shared her views on her school and about feeling less important than Sam. Elaine was very grateful that Izzy had spoken to her rather than bottling it up and it coming out in 'teenage' behaviour. This way Elaine was able to sustain a connection with her daughter and help her solve the problems with her school. She was also able to see what Izzy needed from her and respond to that need. Izzy felt her words empowered her. It's so much easier when kids are able to put into words what they are feeling, but before they can do that for themselves we have to be experts at guessing or deducing what they might be experiencing. Every time we consider what it's like for them, they get a powerful message that people care, consider and try to understand others' experiences. That's a powerful attitude for our children to take into adulthood.

Elaine's reflections

1. Transitioning to secondary school is another key milestone in a child's life. Are you concerned about how they will cope? How did you, or how are you going to, prepare them for the transition?

2. Most children are exposed to online pornography by their early teenage years. Have you had the conversation with them about what your rules and values are on this subject?

3. Emotional intelligence is at the heart of being a successful adult. Being able to articulate and discuss your feelings with others is key in managing emotions.

How do you help your child name their emotions in order to be able to manage them better?

4. What support, if any, does your child access at school? If you are concerned about your child's educational attainment or social skills, your SENCO is a good place to start, and getting a good educational psychology assessment can prove very useful.

5. If your child struggles with written exams, have you considered applying for special dispensation in their exams, such as extra time, a reader or scribe, or a laptop for writing?

Further reading

Daniel Goleman, *Emotional Intelligence: Why It Can Matter More than IQ*, 2009.

Daniel Goleman, *What Makes a Leader: Why Emotional Intelligence Matters*, 2014.

John M. Gottman and Joan DeClaire, *Raising an Emotionally Intelligent Child: The Heart of Parenting*, 1998.

Laura Markham, *Peaceful Parent, Happy Kids: How to Stop Yelling and Start Connecting*, 2013.

7

Moving On Up

(Sixth Form)

It is time we lost the stigma around dyslexia. It is not a disadvantage; it is merely a different way of thinking.

Sir Richard Branson, business magnate,
investor and philanthropist

The GCSE syllabus was brutal. So many subjects, so much information to learn! But Sam's mindset had changed. He no longer saw himself as a failure, and started to become a happy, motivated learner. For the past ten years, we and everyone who supported Sam had been contributing to changing his mindset from a fixed one to one of growth. Carol Dweck, a professor of psychology at Stanford University, eloquently defines the difference:

In a fixed mindset students believe their basic abilities, their intelligence, their talents, are just fixed traits. They have a certain amount and that's that, and then their goal becomes to look smart all the time and never look dumb. In a growth mindset, students understand that their talents and abilities can be developed through effort, good teaching and persistence. They don't necessarily think everyone's the same or anyone can be Einstein, but they believe everyone can get smarter if they work at it.

Sam now believed that with application, effort and the right attitude, he could develop his natural capabilities and talents. He'd already failed spectacularly in his early life, and given the way we helped him cope with any mistakes he made or failure he experienced, he was always keen to give things a go.

He started to understand that although he may never conquer his dyslexia, there was nothing to stop him from conquering the world!

The hypersensitivity that had been at the root of so many of his outbursts remains in Sam to this day, his senses on alert all the time. But he started using it to his advantage. As he was driving me somewhere recently, he asked if I'd spotted the Aston Martin DB7 behind us. 'No, Sam,' I replied, 'I haven't got eyes in the back of my head.' But he explained he'd recognised the car only from the sound of its engine. From his hypersensitive trait he'd developed an impressive attention to detail. A superpower.

Sam was at last surrounded by people who believed in him, and his teachers inspired him. In turn, he respected his teachers for caring so deeply and passionately about their students.

Unlocking potential

August is the month for exam results. We were on holiday in the gorgeous East Neuk of Fife, and I'd tossed and turned all night. Sam's GCSE results were coming via snail mail. We waited in all morning with no sign of the postie. The tension was mounting and we were all getting a bit snappy, so Tony, Izzy and I decided to head out and blow the cobwebs away on the golf course, leaving Sam in peace to wait for the mail to be delivered.

After a couple of hours, as we came up to the tenth hole, we spotted Sam sitting alone on the rocky crag overlooking the green, looking reflective. We waved to him and he scrambled down like a mountain goat, announcing the news. 'I've got eight GCSEs ... one A, three Bs and four Cs.'

Never in our wildest dreams had Tony or I imagined this would be the outcome. We felt such a huge sense of achievement and were brimming with pride for Sam. We erupted into celebration, whooping, dancing and congratulating, our raucous jubilation echoing across the Firth of Forth.

Sam, however, seemed a little disappointed. I was so surprised. He confessed he'd been hoping for a few more A grades.

I then realised how far we'd all come. My son was not going to accept second best. He wanted more. He had a desire to achieve, to succeed, and his dyslexia was not going to stop him.

Today, Sam still feels the burning ambition that propelled him through those two years:

I'd been told over the entire course of my education that I'd never sit GCSEs, and I just wanted to prove everyone wrong. I was at a stage where I was able to study what I wanted to study, and I stepped up a gear for my final two years at school.

He began to become known for his ability to think laterally and strategically. Along with several other pupils, Sam was asked to represent the school in the Surrey Problem-Solving Challenge, a competition for all the eleven- to eighteen-year-old students in the county. Teams of six are set a problem to solve within a fixed time, using only the materials provided.

Sam explains what happens in these competitions:

You'd be given these challenges, where all you had was some really basic raw materials like paper, glue and sticky tape, and you had to design, say, a go-kart, or a windmill that powered something, or perhaps a lift. In the lift challenge, you had to make a freestanding structure that could lift a packet of mints to the height of the table. Points were awarded for the number of mints that could be lifted, with bonus points for lifting them all in a set time limit. More House students – with our dyslexic traits – excelled at these tasks, and for three years in a row I headed up the team and always got them through to the finals! I'm not sure I was the most creative brain in the team, but I did become quite a good leader. I was good at bringing

people together around the table, identifying their skill sets, and get-
ting the best out of them.

I'm sure Sam's adeptness as a leader is due, in part, to some of the parenting techniques we'd used at home. Descriptive praise and emotion coaching have definitely had an impact on the way Sam and Izzy communicate with others. They now both influence others through the power of their words.

Sam recognises he's good at giving others descriptive praise:

It's ironic, because I don't really like it when you use it with me – you always speak in your Parent Practice voice – but I know it works. I'm probably not even conscious I'm doing it these days, as it's so deeply ingrained in me to look for the positives in people and look for their attitude and effort and the progress they make. I realise now that the communication skills I use with other people are those skills that have been used with me.

Tides turn

After their GCSEs, many of Sam's cohort moved off to further education colleges, and Angus went out into the real world to train as a brickie. Sam felt the pressure to move on too, and was sceptical about staying on in such a small sixth form – More House had only fifty boys in the whole year group. However, after much reflection, he decided to stay.

Sam had developed an exemplary work ethic, both in and out of school, and he managed to secure his first summer holiday job as a car park attendant at the 2012 Wimbledon Championships. Only sixteen years old, he was one of the youngest staff members there. This was his first proper job, complete with long shifts and painfully early mornings to get to Wimbledon for a 6.30 a.m. start. He loved every moment.

He couldn't believe his luck when he was given the debenture holders' car park, which meant he'd frequently be passed by the wealthiest and most famous guests, many of whom were chauffeured in impressive cars. Sam always managed to talk to the drivers and often negotiated his way into the back of a sumptuous, leather-clad Bentley, whiling away the afternoon watching the tennis coverage on the personal TV screens, in the lap of luxury.

One day he came home breathless with excitement, jolting me out of a rare moment of relaxation in the garden. 'Mum, Mum! Guess what happened today!'

I sat up and took a sip of my G&T, looking forward to hearing about how, perhaps, he'd met Andy Murray, or spotted David Beckham, or …

'I drove the latest Nissan Qashqai!'

I nearly choked on an ice cube. 'Pardon?' (I'd heard him perfectly well.) 'But you don't even have a licence – how did …?'

'Well, my boss just asked me if I could drive, so I said yes.' His eyes glinted. 'He never asked me if I had a driving licence!'

Now, if that diagnosis of Asperger's syndrome that Sam had borne for most of his childhood had actually been true, he would have been excused for answering his boss's question literally, but I knew exactly what he was doing. He has a rebellious streak, and if he can get away with breaking a rule or two, he will. Of course, for a complete petrolhead, this had been an irresistible opportunity to drive an amazing car. And unbeknown to me, he knew perfectly well how to drive after all those weekends driving the Land Rover around the farm! He assured me he'd only driven the Qashqai around an empty car park. As I imagined him there, doing laps in someone else's big, expensive, brand-new car, I took another sip of my gin to stop myself laughing aloud. I didn't want to encourage Sam to break more rules. But I was secretly in admiration of my sixteen-year-old, who now had such confidence, was starting to live his life on his own terms, and was loving it.

His first taste of earning his own money that summer quickly led to another job as a barista when the new term started in autumn, serving coffees and teas at the tearooms on Wimbledon Common. Every Sunday, he soldiered through a gruelling nine-hour shift, on his feet all day, working in a crowded space and dealing with demanding customers.

There's a lot of dignity in working, regardless of role or remuneration. Sam began to develop a sense of pride in earning money, and before long he'd started to think up ways to make money on his own terms. He set up a little business at school, selling noodles at lunchtime. He'd discovered that pots of instant noodles, which cost 20p in the local Asian supermarket, could be sold for quite a profit to hungry pupils and teachers. He seized the opportunity, and trundled off to school with a small suitcase. Despite the questionable nutritional value of a pot of noodles full of monosodium glutamate, and the fact that he was probably breaking many a school rule, the teachers turned a blind eye!

Sam had become excellent at managing his time, juggling weekend work and the lunchtime business with his A level studies. His chosen subjects of art, product design and business studies were perfect for him. He was interested in and excited about them all, and motivated to learn.

The end of the lower sixth came round quickly, marked by Founder's Day, a huge celebration of each school year. This year, it fell on one of the hottest days on record. More than a thousand guests filed into endless rows of seats in an enormous marquee. We were familiar with the long and punishing schedule, starting with the fundraising auction, then the governor and Mr Huggett each gave speeches, which were followed by prize-giving and finally the head boy's and senior prefects' addresses, in which they announced the next head boy. Then we'd all scramble to the terrace for some strawberries and cream and a glass or two of Prosecco.

After two hours in the sweltering tent, it was time for the head boy and senior prefects to speak. It was always a real delight to hear the boys talk about where they'd come from and who they are today and, by the end, there was rarely a dry eye in the house. I was almost dozing in the heat when I heard 'Sam Halligan'. Tony elbowed me back into reality.

'What's happening?' I whispered.

'Sam's just been made next year's head boy!'

I felt completely overwhelmed. How on earth had we got here? From a boy who'd been excluded from three schools and written off by society, to a confident young man chosen by teachers and fellow pupils to lead his school in his final year. I felt the deepest joy and such tremendous pride. But something I couldn't quite grasp was happening. People were congratulating *us* – his parents – and I realised the tide had finally turned. No longer were we social pariahs with an unacceptable child. After all these years, all our efforts, our relentless determination and our unfailing belief in Sam, everyone could see the diamond. But of course it wasn't down to us alone. It had been a concerted group effort. Team Sam comprised us, his inspirational teachers, his compassionate head teacher and, most important of all, Sam. He made this happen and he had every right to be bursting with pride at his latest achievement.

Growing wings

Sam says of himself:

I was the working man's head boy. I challenged some of the pomp and ceremony that previous captains had created. For me, it was key that I was approachable, not aloof, so the first thing I did was scrap the ritual of the head boy and prefects sitting on golden chairs during assembly. That was just unnecessarily special and created barriers to communication. We weren't kings! You've got to be on the ground, mingling. You can't stay at the top of the ladder, otherwise people are not going to tell you what's going on, and you need to know what's going on in order to lead effectively.

And so, for the next year, Sam led. He represented the school, became the liaison point between students and the head of sixth form, and represented the pupil body during the opening of the impressive new engineering block – together with Richard Rogers, one of the architects who designed the Pompidou Centre in Paris!

Sam did apply to a handful of universities as he was keen on studying real estate management. He received an offer from Oxford Brookes University, conditional on him attaining an A, B and C in his A levels. But he sensed university may not be right for him, given how hard he found the traditional learning environment. He also doubted he would get the grades.

When Founder's Day came around again, in the summer of 2014, it heralded the end of Sam's school education. The marquee awaited us. Sam, knowing he would be giving his head boy speech, had chosen his outfit carefully: bright banana-yellow trousers. Now here was a young man comfortable in his own skin! He had rehearsed his speech and was well prepared. But as he walked onto the stage and took over the lectern from Mr Huggett, standing in front of more than a thousand pairs of eyes – waiting – all was silent.

My heart sank. He must have had stage fright. Had he forgotten his words? Was he anxious about reading out loud? Then, very calmly, he picked up Mr Huggett's glass of water and took a long, cool drink. He was in no hurry. At last he announced, 'That's better. It's pretty hot in here, isn't it?'

The marquee erupted in laughter. Without even realising it, Sam had just delivered the perfect ice-breaker, and warmed up his audience naturally. The speech brought tears to our eyes as it beautifully encapsulated the journey he'd been on, and how vitally important it is to find personalised, differentiated, and forward-thinking educational provision.

Here is a transcript of Sam's Founder's Day speech.

I started at More House in January 2009. On day three, I ran away. (I'm sure Mrs Stiff has not forgotten.) On day five, I locked myself in the staff toilet. (Mr Williamson negotiated me out of that one.) Today, I am honoured to stand here as school captain.

And now, let me tell you a story about an eighteen-year-old boy in his final year at school. He's received a university offer conditional upon him gaining an A, B and C in his A levels. Why is this remarkable? Well, he had a very tough start to life. He is very dyslexic and was diagnosed with oppositional defiant disorder (ODD). He felt very different and thought he was a bad person. He was a very angry young boy. His parents struggled with him and received much conflicting advice. They tried many possible solutions without success.

Travelling on public transport was a complete nightmare. He was all over the place. It was sometimes dangerous and always embarrassing. He'd been to three schools by age seven — and had been excluded from all of them. One school had been so unable to manage him, they locked him in a cupboard.

Luckily, his parents did not give up on him. Parents never give up on their children, but sometimes they accept there are limits to what can be achieved. They took positive parenting courses and trained hard to help him. They researched different therapies to support him. But most of all, they never gave up on the picture they had of who he could be. I do not mean they wanted him to be a scholar or an athlete or a musician or to follow any particular career path; but they knew he was a good and capable person. They found schools that could support him, and it became possible for him to attend school because of all the work they put in at home. He's progressed well over the years. He has always had drive and self-belief that I think comes from his parents' belief in him. He may not achieve those ABC university grades — but do not bet against him — he keeps pushing past the boundaries of what was thought possible.

Reading and writing are still a struggle for him, but this young man will not be stopped by that. I am told he has great resilience and maturity, well beyond his years. I'm also told his social skills are very acute and he has an insight about people that is rare in someone his age. What has worked has been ten years of positive encouragement, allowing him to have responsibility, fostering independence, giving him an understanding and acceptance of his feelings of difference, anxieties, frustrations and anger, and helping him learn from failure and bounce back from setbacks.

One thing this family do is spend time together, whether playing golf or just enjoying family barbecues.

This boy has developed passions outside of school that have helped his sense of achievement. There are no glass ceilings when your sense of self-worth is strong.

He may not be a doctor or a lawyer, but he will lead a productive and fulfilling life, doing the best he is capable of.

Surely this is every parent's dream for their children.

If you hadn't already worked it out, I am that eighteen-year-old boy. And during my time at More House, and many other schools, I have realised one thing – whatever you do in life, as long as you follow your passion, you can overcome any difficulties that may have held you back.

In life, do the things you are passionate about – not just good at!

Parents: if you want your sons to succeed, let them follow their passions.

This may come as a surprise to my parents and many of my teachers, but I've been reading a book …

(Here, the audience burst into laughter again. Sam smiled, and continued.)

I've been reading a book during the past two weeks, while enjoying the sunshine at the Wimbledon Championships.

This book – Screw It, Let's Do It *– was written by Richard Branson.*

Branson started his first business at age fifteen, publishing a school magazine in the sixth form, called Student. *At the time, he did not view this as a business but as a means of spreading his passion for political news. With his parents' support, he was able to follow his passion rather than the preordained career paths followed by most of his peers.*

For those who've been counting, I have used the word 'passion' five times in the past thirty seconds. It is that important to me.

I have many people to thank.

All my teachers and fellow pupils for supporting me, but especially:

Mrs Rouse – on behalf of the 3D crew – for feeding our growing appetites and encouraging my use of creativity outside the art room.

Mr Morgan – for building our independent spirit and looking beyond just the grades, while appreciating that everyone has a different learning style.

Mr Kirkham – for guiding me through my sixth form captaincy and inspiring my interest in English, a subject so far removed from my comfort zone.

Mr Rashleigh – for putting up with the loud mobs playing table football outside your office, but appreciating this is an integral part of sixth form life.

Mr Babbage – for stepping in and building my confidence while mentoring me through my business studies. Your tireless efforts are really appreciated. Keep working on that golf handicap though! I guarantee it will start to come down.

Miss Burn – for being an excellent mediator between Jamie's grumbles and the rest of the form.

Mr Williams – for managing the PE misfit form in Year 11 and not saving George when he was attacked by two gymnastic mats. This may have been endorsed by other members of the year group, but we'll never know.

Above all, to my parents – for supporting me through the ups and downs I've just described. It's been a rollercoaster ride.

And finally, Mr Huggett – congratulations on your OBE for your tireless dedication to education and your belief that all pupils deserve a second, and third, chance. But most of all, for believing in me.

Thank you, and good luck in following your passions.

Melissa says: The importance of creating happy, motivated learners

Some children go through all their school days hating school, or if not hating it then just tolerating it. That was certainly true of Sam's early school life. These kids are not happy in that environment and don't enjoy learning. Many will have learning difficulties, like Sam. But Sam's story tells us that a learning difficulty doesn't have to stop children from enjoying learning and progressing to fulfil whatever their potential is and achieving. My two sons are moderately dyslexic. They went to different schools and had completely different experiences there which resulted in one's self-esteem being badly battered while the other was able to handle failures and feel competent.

If children are to do their best at school, and thereafter, they need to be self-motivated and believe they are capable, to try things and take risks, to work hard and persevere, to have self-control, courage and drive and be willing to follow their dreams, perhaps trying a different path to that taken by the majority. They need to be curious and think creatively. It will help if they think of themselves as learners and problem-solvers. They need to be resilient, to not be defeated by failures but to embrace them as opportunities for growth.

Parents and teachers can help children develop these attitudes and qualities by:

- Building strong self-esteem, with a realistic sense of their abilities and capacities. We can encourage risk-taking and persistence, build resilience, encourage thinking for themselves and willingness to challenge ideas (this can be uncomfortable for adults) by what we pay attention to and how we speak to our children and students. (This is descriptive praise, which we looked at in Chapter 5. We'll look at how it applies to schooling here.)

- Teaching children how to respond well to failures and mistakes, by our modelling and by how we speak about failures and also by teaching children how their brains work.

- Being really aware of what values we are communicating, especially around success and results in academia, sports and extracurricular activities. Are we expecting other non-performance-related qualities like kindness and respect?

Parents can also give children opportunities to develop creative and independent thinking by:

- Avoiding overscheduling so that they can have time just to be, to play, to explore and to reflect, as well as have family time.

- Providing toys and activities that challenge and allow freedom – children with learning difficulties particularly need to be able to engage in activities where they can be successful.

- Limiting time in front of a screen.

- Not jumping in to solve problems for them.

We can also help motivate our children by showing an interest. Talk to them about what they're learning – enthuse about science, history, literature and show how what they're learning is relevant in life – e.g. maths skills in cooking, shopping and sudoku. Read books, theirs and yours, and take them to museums, art galleries and places of interest. Know your child's teachers and timetable – show that their education is important to you. Boys particularly need to see dads involved in their learning – read with them, supervise homework and go to school functions.

How else can we motivate? When we praise our children descriptively we are painting a picture of who they are and what they are capable of. We need to encourage them to think of themselves as learners, thinkers and problem-solvers, people who can take risks and be creative. For example: 'You figured out how to make your model stronger. That was very creative.'

Elaine mentioned the work of Carol Dweck. Her studies have shown that the way we praise has an impact on children's attitudes to learning. She demonstrates that conventional praise, with its emphasis on cleverness and results, is actually damaging. She found that children praised for intelligence perform less well on tasks, are less motivated and enjoy the task less than children who are praised for effort.

Our society worships talent, and many people assume that possessing superior intelligence or ability ... is a recipe for success. In fact ... more than 35 years of scientific investigation suggests that an overemphasis on intellect or talent leaves people vulnerable to failure, fearful of challenges and unwilling to remedy their shortcomings.

Elaine referred to the two views of intelligence identified by Dweck: helpless versus mastery-oriented. People with a helpless view or 'fixed mindset' believe that you have only a finite amount of intelligence. Mistakes crack their self-confidence because they attribute errors to a lack of ability, which they feel powerless to change. They avoid challenges because challenges make mistakes more likely. Students who hold a fixed mindset have negative views of effort, believing that having to work hard at something is a sign of low ability. They think that a person with talent or intelligence does not need to work hard to do well.

The mastery-oriented students, on the other hand, think intelligence is malleable and can be developed through education and hard work. They believe that they can expand their intellectual skills and want to learn. Because slip-ups stem from a lack of effort, not ability, they can be remedied by more effort. Students with a growth mindset react to problems positively. One student, in the face of difficulty, pulled up his chair, rubbed his hands together, smacked his lips and said, 'I love a challenge!' Another, also confronting hard problems, looked up at the experimenter and approvingly declared, 'I was hoping this would be informative!'

So don't call your children clever. Instead say: 'You are trying really hard' or something about the strategies the child is employing. For example: 'The way you've set out your numbers in neat rows makes it more likely that you'll get the adding up right.' 'When you didn't know what that term meant you went to the science dictionary to look it up – you didn't give up.'

When we praise we prioritise the behaviour or quality we're paying attention to. If we pay attention only to achievements, results or scores, children learn that results-based success is what counts. When they do not achieve the result hoped for, are our children not worthwhile?

When your child comes home from a netball/football match don't let your first question be 'Did you win?', but 'How was the game? Did you play well? Did the coach have any tips about shooting? Were you able to set up some goals? How did the team play together?' Make sure you praise areas outside the academic, sporting and musical arenas as well – praise behaviour and examples of character traits that you value (such as honesty, kindness or good communication) that are not so closely related to success in performance areas. We don't want to give them the idea that our approval is dependent on their achievements.

Elaine and Tony and Sam's teachers were helping Sam develop a growth mindset. Paradoxically, by emphasising qualities rather than results, Sam was able to attain greater achievements.

All of us fail. Children with learning difficulties or special needs, like Sam, will have trouble achieving things that other kids do more easily. The adults in their lives need to help these children identify what successes they do have and we need to teach them that failures don't diminish a person but show us where we can improve.

We need our kids to not be afraid of challenges. We can teach them that neural pathways are formed not by doing easy things but by taking on challenges, where there is a risk of failure.

Although children should not be shielded from failures, it's not enough just to drop them into situations where they will fail and to cover their work in red ink. Failing by itself does not promote resilience. We have to actively teach kids emotional intelligence and we have to be mindful about how we approach failure, regarding it as an opportunity to learn.

In order to get children used to the idea of doing their best, making improvements and not being afraid of mistakes when approaching schoolwork and music/sports practice, I suggest parents adopt the following approach routinely:

- first find several positive things to descriptively praise (comment on content or presentation, focus, attitude, effort, improvement made or strategies used);

- then ask your child to find something to improve; and

- keep the ratio of positive comments to improvements at 5:1.

Model handling your own failures positively – there should be lots of opportunities! When you make a mistake don't beat yourself up about it, but acknowledge the mistake and, if possible, why it was a mistake. Then, where appropriate, take steps to remedy it or make repairs. Articulate what you are learning and show that you are not diminished by your failures but can profit from them. For example:

This morning when we were getting ready for school I yelled at you guys. We were in such a hurry and I didn't think you were being very helpful in getting your uniforms on. It's not a good idea for me to yell at you as it doesn't make you, or me, feel good, and it doesn't make things go any faster.

I'm sorry.

I thought about it afterwards and realised that I yelled because we were in a hurry and I didn't want to be late. I was anxious and frustrated. Tomorrow I am going to make sure we get started earlier and I'm going to see what I can do tonight so that there's less to do in the morning. Hopefully, I learned something from this.

Elaine's reflections

1. Children with a growth mindset have a desire to learn, embrace challenges and persist in the face of setbacks. They learn from feedback and understand that struggles provide opportunities for us to grow. What mindset does your child have?

2. Good teachers can play a hugely important role in influencing your child to achieve their potential. Can you identify any key influencers in your child's life?

3. Working part-time or having a summer job instils confidence and can boost self-esteem no matter how menial the task, as there is dignity in work. Can you identify any work opportunities, paid or voluntary, that would suit your child?

4. Speaking in front of an audience, playing a musical instrument or performing on stage in a production requires tremendous courage and confidence. Think of a time when your child has surprised you with their bravery and reflect on the words you used to let them know they should feel proud of themselves.

5. In his Founder's Day speech, Sam spoke of the importance of finding your passion in life. Identifying this enables you to set goals, which in turn gives you resilience and focus. Can you identify what your child's passion could be?

Further reading

Richard Branson, Richard Branson: Dyslexia Is Merely Another Way of Thinking, *The Times* [blog], 2017 (30 April). Available at: https://www.thetimes.co.uk/article/richard-branson-dyslexia-is-merely-another-way-of-thinking-8tlmgsndw.

Richard Branson, *Screw It, Let's Do It: Lessons in Life*, 2011.

Carol S. Dweck, *Mindset: Changing the Way You Think to Fulfil Your Potential*, updated edition, 2017.

Carol S. Dweck, The Secret to Raising Smart Kids, *Scientific American*, 2015 (1 January). Available at: https://www. scientificamerican.com/article/the-secret-to-raising-smart-kids1/.

James Morehead, Stanford University's Carol Dweck on the Growth Mindset and Education, *OneDublin.org*, 2012 (19 June). Available at: https://onedublin.org/2012/06/19/stanford-universitys-carol-dweck-on-the-growth-mindset-and-education/.

8

Anything Is Possible

(Adulthood)

All parenting turns on a crucial question: to what extent parents should accept their children for who they are, and to what extent they should help them become their best selves.

Andrew Solomon, author of *Far from the Tree*

The end of Sam's time at More House was bittersweet as, despite finishing on a real high with his Founder's Day speech, he'd caught a virus and been too ill to sit the final part of his A level business studies paper. He'd prepared well, and was enthused about the topic, which was all about emerging markets in China and the trade relationship with the UK.

Around the same time, Sam had heard about a local young entrepreneur, Matt Turner, who'd been the only boy in his year group to have finished school at eighteen but not gone to university. Within eight years, Matt had built up a successful event management business. He, like his business, was quirky, energetic, different and refreshing; Sam loved this. He dropped a line to Matt explaining that he was just about to leave school, wasn't sure what he wanted to do next as university didn't feel right for him, and that he'd love to meet up and explore opportunities.

They got on like a house on fire and, within twenty-four hours of meeting, Sam had been offered a permanent position as head of events at Clownfish Events.

'I just knew this was what I wanted to do,' says Sam.

Something fresh and different. After this meeting, I felt a huge sense of relief that I'd found something I was really excited about. But after all the work leading up to my A levels, and with the end in sight, I guess the massive dose of adrenaline from it all just made me crash and burn. I spent the next five days in bed with a nasty virus and ended up missing my final business studies paper.

But it didn't matter. As soon as Sam was well enough, he began driving the length and breadth of England for corporate events, with everything in the back of the van from rodeo bulls to surf simulators, snow globes to human table football, and the ultimate in wedding party kit – the photo booth. He learned how to manage clients and team members, work in a team, and plan and negotiate his way around the country. He met executives from the biggest companies in the world, from the BBC to Google. It was edgy and exciting, and he was earning his first proper salary, so felt motivated. The job combined everything he was good at – meeting people, setting up technical equipment and, of course, driving. It was the perfect combination.

It also opened Sam's eyes to the sacrifices you have to make when running your own business. Long hours, no social life, and working every weekend. With a temporary staff of about a hundred to look after, there was so much responsibility. Sam gained invaluable insights into how to run a small business.

He got his A level results in August 2014. Results day is always a tricky time; you just never know the outcome, and so many dreams are made and shattered on that day. But Sam was relaxed about it. He was working at Clownfish, enjoying life, and university was not the be-all and end-all for him. And yet, as he opened the envelope and scanned down the letter, we learned he'd achieved the A, B and C grades he needed to go to university. Once again, he'd defied belief. However, he'd been undecided about the benefit of university from the start. It was a huge financial commitment, and not necessarily the right path for him, so he decided to defer his place until the following year, giving him time to decide and keeping his options open.

After a year at Clownfish, Sam felt his time there had run its course and he stepped down, ready to tackle new challenges.

The Italian Job and the Mongol Rally

Aged nineteen, Sam decided to go on a road trip to Italy with Elliott McTaggart. They wanted to try their hand at picking up some old classic cars and selling them on. They borrowed a Land Rover from the farm, hired a trailer, and off they went with Sam's hard-earned cash.

I thought they were crazy. They didn't speak the lingo, they knew nothing about importing cars and they were certainly no mechanics, so how would they even know what they were buying? But I underestimated Sam's love of cars, his ambition to run his own business, and his ability to learn anything just by watching online videos and specialist car programmes! I was amazed at how knowledgeable he'd become about classic cars. He'd identified that the only one he could afford to buy was the Fiat Cinquecento Lusso (1968–1972), and he'd found a couple of 1969 models for sale in a remote part of northern Italy, somewhere near Milan.

Four days later, they arrived back home with a couple of beauties. (Cinquecentos, of course – a bright yellow one and a white one.)

Within a week, they'd made their first sale and turned over a profit of 300 per cent. This was Sam's first taste of trading, and he was hooked. Not just on making a sale; his love affair with anything on four wheels had developed into an enduring passion for classic cars. Today, as excited about them as ever, Sam runs a successful and growing classic motor dealership.

Sam loved that brief road trip so much that he decided he wanted to do more. Within days, he told me he'd signed up for the Mongol Rally with Angus and Angus's girlfriend. I went to have a look at the website to see what it was all about.

It appeared to be organised by a group called the Adventurists.
I read on:

Welcome to the Mongol Rally: the greatest motoring adventure on the
planet. The Mongol Rally thunders 10,000 miles across the moun-
tains, desert and steppe of Europe and Asia each summer. There's
no backup, no support and no set route; just you, your fellow adven-
turists and a tiny car you bought from a scrapyard for £11.50. If
nothing goes wrong, everything has gone wrong. Bollocks to tarmac,
ABS and gadgets that help you find your navel. The Mongol Rally
is about getting lost, using your long-neglected wits, raising shedloads
of cash for charity and scraping into the finish line with your vehicle
in tatters and a wild grin smeared across your grubby face. Neither
your car, nor your life, will ever be the same again.

The rules of the Rally are gloriously simple:

1. You can only take a farcically small vehicle.

2. You're completely on your own.

3. You've got to raise £1,000 for charity.

I felt the blood drain from my face as I scrolled down the
page. This wasn't just risky. It was mad.

The boys wanted to drive from London, through twenty-
two countries in Europe, ferry the car across the Caspian Sea,
through most of the 'stan countries, and finally arrive at Ulan
Ude, the capital of the Republic of Buryatia, in Siberia. The
logistics of arranging visas was already mind-bogglingly
complicated, not to mention the expected run-ins with often-
corrupt traffic police and border controls.

And they wanted to do it in a 1.2 litre Skoda.

My anxiety levels shot through the roof, and that was
before I realised they'd be in territories with no mobile phone
signal! There'd be no way of contacting anyone for help if
they got into trouble. I was seriously concerned about the
risks of such an adventure. Sam told me how he intended to
prepare for the trip, and that Angus was going as the car
mechanic. Tony and I had several conversations late into the

night and he reminded me that by the time I was Sam's age, I was travelling independently every year to the USA to work at a summer camp, and that three years later I'd travelled to South Africa, again on my own, so the adventurist spirit was certainly in Sam's genes! Sam was independent, and a problem-solver, and I knew that preventing him from going on the trip wasn't going to work. The best thing we could do was support him and help him set up for success.

I convinced Sam that the only way I'd give him my blessing to do this was if he promised to hire a satellite phone. He agreed. They called themselves Team Nomad.

They immediately set up a website and a Facebook page to begin raising the required sponsorship money. Next, they bought a 2008 Skoda Fabia on eBay, which, to my relief, was in great condition. Angus had vetted it and found it to be sound, before he dismantled it to rebuild the suspension and make it driveable across the desert plains of Mongolia, where usually only those with four-wheel drives would venture. Once the sponsorship started to come in, they got the car wrapped with sponsorship logos.

In July 2015, fully prepared and itching to go, Team Nomad departed from the McTaggart farm to join the starting party at Goodwood Racecourse. From that point on, we had to rely on their blog posts for any updates.

It was the longest, quietest seven weeks of my life.

The rest of us headed up to Fife for the month of August. It started off as a welcome distraction, but we all ended up obsessed with following the updates on the Adventurists' blog, Team Nomad's own blog, and any other sites we knew of from the two hundred plus teams taking part.

Three weeks in, one of the teams' cars crashed and exploded, and worry gripped my chest. All I could do was hope and pray that our boys would return home safely.

Their car broke down in Mongolia. They'd been driving across the hot, rocky expanse and hadn't seen a tarmac road for days or any sign of civilisation. They'd picked up another Mongol rallyer on the way and were helping her get to the next town when the Skoda hit a boulder and punctured the fuel pump. Even Angus, with all his expertise, had admitted defeat. Soon they had no fuel and were low on water. They knew that people could die in this wilderness. The silence around them was as alarming as the silence within the team. (The group dynamics were 'problematic'.) No one had passed them for four hours, and the sun was starting to set.

As they were beginning to lose hope, they spotted a cloud of dust on the horizon. It moved closer, and an old Suzuki wagon finally came clattering out of it. The boys jumped into the path of the vehicle, shouting and gesticulating frantically. The car ground to a halt, kicking up a load more dust, and a local got out to see what the fuss was. Technically, the wagon shouldn't have been able to tow the Skoda, but a few Mongolian tugriks (the national currency) did the trick! It was their salvation.

Within minutes, the wagon drove onto the first tarmac road they'd seen in days; then a town emerged from over the hill. They'd had absolutely no idea that they'd broken down just four miles away from civilisation, and a garage.

....

They eventually completed the rally. Where many others had failed, these three nineteen-year-olds succeeded, with grit, resilience and resourcefulness.

In the process, they had raised a whopping £5,000 for Cool Earth, a charity that works alongside indigenous villages to halt rainforest destruction. Little did they know what good fortune their charitable endeavours would later bring.

The Rickshaw Run

The Adventurists were certainly right – Sam came back from Mongolia a changed person. The experience had turbo-boosted his confidence, showing him it was worth giving things a go even if there was a risk of failing. With this, university was back on the cards. He decided to take up his deferred place at Oxford Brookes, but made a bold request to transfer from the project management course he'd been accepted onto the more demanding BSc in real estate management, which he'd always preferred. 'I always knew I wanted to do a job that would involve some creative thinking,' he explains, 'and somehow add value, whether that be economically or socially.'

The problem was that the entry requirements for the BSc were higher than the grades he'd received. But he had become gutsy and bold, able to ask for something that not long ago would have seemed an impassable obstacle.

He was accepted.

His gap year of work and adventure had a huge impact on his maturity and outlook, and enabled him to think deeply and meaningfully about his future. After seeing the change in him, I now strongly recommend a year out to everyone who's thinking about it, instead of simply following a path set out by others. I believe that those students who are able to take some time out after school, whether to travel, work or undertake an apprenticeship, will enter into the next period of their lives with more clarity and vision for their own future.

Sam started university in the autumn of 2015. He soon became a bit of a pied piper, drawing people in and quickly building up a fabulous group of friends. The written word remains hard for Sam to this day, but the university was incredibly supportive of his learning needs. He still has a reader and a scribe in his exams, and a dedicated learning support tutor to help with things like essay planning, note organisation and CV preparation. Plus, with technological advances in the upgrading of tools such as voice recognition programmes, literacy has never been so well supported.

Sam settled into his first term, enjoying university life and knuckling down to study. He was just getting into studying the finer points of property management and building design when he received an email telling him he'd won a trip to the Peruvian rainforest. Cool Earth, the charity he'd fundraised for during the Mongol Rally, had entered him into a draw – I say draw, but it was actually a snail race, each snail representing a team from the Mongol Rally, powering along at centimetres per hour to reach the finish line. As it happened, the winning snail represented Team Nomad!

They had secured themselves an all-expenses-paid twelve-day excursion to the Peruvian jungle to live with the Ashaninka tribe. It was a trip of a lifetime. They would go downriver into the heart of the jungle, which remained untouched by regular tourists. It was in the middle of his first year at university, and it wasn't going to be an easy trip. It was dangerous; the bitter, ongoing drug war in Peru had reached a nearby area, leading to a spate of deaths in the area. To Sam, it was a no-brainer; he agreed without hesitation in his usual impulsive manner. Tony and I, however, were lukewarm in our response. Taking time off university, when the teaching hours were already so limited, seemed like a crazy thing to do.

'How are you going to catch up on missed lectures and team assignments, Sam?' I asked. 'Are you going to tell your course tutor? How are you going to meet coursework deadlines in the middle of the Amazon jungle?'

Sam, ever pragmatic, replied, 'Chillax, Mum. I can sort it. I'll let my course tutor know. This is a trip of a lifetime, and if I don't take this opportunity I'll always regret not doing it.' He had a point.

However, Angus was now no longer seeing his girlfriend, so the boys, armed with their usual gumption and nerve, managed to negotiate that the spare place be given to Angus's brother Elliott. So in March 2016, Sam, Angus and Elliott went out to Peru to experience something quite extraordinary. He came back in one piece, although he'd managed to slice off the tip of his index finger with a machete. With blood everywhere, they had sewn it back together using their makeshift first aid kit, with nothing but a bottle of vodka and biting down on a piece of wood as pain relief. Sam has a remarkably high pain threshold. 'It was pretty sore,' he admitted. He still has nerve damage in the finger but just lives with it. 'It hasn't impacted my golf swing too much!'

....

The Peruvian trip heightened his desire to travel even more. The next challenge he wanted to undertake was the Rickshaw Run that August – another crazy challenge from the Adventurists involving driving 2,500 miles from north to south India in an auto-rickshaw. Except this time, Sam would not be taking his mates.

He'd be taking his sister and his mother.

I'm still not sure what made me sign up to this. Perhaps turning fifty and having a mini midlife crisis. Or maybe my own impulsive and adventurous side, put on hold for the past two decades, had been reignited by Sam's recent escapades. But within a matter of weeks, we'd established Team Taj Ma'Halligan, created the design for our auto-rickshaw, and signed up to join seventy-four other teams on the starting line in Shillong, northern India.

Once we'd actually started planning it, the reality of the situation dawned on me and the fear set in. My first concern was whether I'd actually fit into the back of a rickshaw … And were these vehicles safe? What speed could they go? Why, exactly, were we doing a dangerous challenge during the monsoon season, crossing areas with known guerrilla army insurgencies? Was I a negligent and reckless mother? One friend casually asked if I had a death wish, which turned me into an anxious wreck.

I got Tony to review our wills.

We did complete the challenge, and I'll leave that story for another time. Suffice to say I was one of the oldest team members, surrounded by youngsters who were all on a mission to have the greatest adventure and see the world. I felt alive, proud of having pushed myself way out of my comfort zone, and was voted Coolest Mum Ever!

But it was the children who really shone, with their resourcefulness and independence. Traversing India in little more than a lawnmower, with no route, no planned accommodation, and temperatures soaring into the fifties, I witnessed Sam and Izzy in a completely alien place.

The Alphabet Kid we once knew was now a world away. Watching him connect with others easily, shop resourcefully for spark plugs and cable ties, and negotiate with everyone from local citizens to traffic police, I finally knew that whatever he did in life, he was going to be okay.

A final message to parents, from Sam

Don't be overly proud. It's not easy to admit something may be wrong with your child. If you think they may have a learning difficulty or a communication issue, identify it early. If they have a problem and it gets overlooked owing to pride, this can have huge implications down the line. Reach out for help and don't feel embarrassed about it.

I was a very sensitive and emotional child. But whenever I got angry or aggressive, I was always remorseful afterwards and what was notable was the way my parents helped me work through it. Don't punish your children. That only makes things worse. Instead, give them the skills and direction to help them make amends and put things right. Don't force your kids to say sorry unless there's meaning to it. The way parents deal with mistakes can actually help their child develop a moral compass.

The key message from me, to you, is this: be curious. Keep exploring, researching and talking to others, because there will usually be signs in the early years that things aren't quite right. If your child is not reaching their developmental milestones, be alert, as it could be an early warning that all may not be well.

At the same time, don't be too quick to bring in the professionals. I know this may sound like a contradiction, as seeking help and support are part of being curious about your child's development, but at the end of the day it's you who will have the greatest influence on your children. Sending your child from professional to professional can leave them wondering what's wrong with them when, in reality, what's missing from the jigsaw could simply be positive parenting.

I would not want to be any other way. Fundamentally, I feel no resentment or sadness about what I've been through, because I am happy with who I am.

Melissa says: The importance of grit and resilience

In all the years I've known Sam, I've consistently been amazed at the way he's progressed. He's always been driven, and has such self-belief that I'm sure comes, not in small part, from his parents' belief in him. Literacy is still a struggle for him, but this young man will not be stopped by that. He has remarkable resilience and a maturity well beyond his years. His acute social skills give him insights about people rarely found in others his age. His ability to understand others' perspectives makes him a very good negotiator. He earned the respect of his peers and teachers, and being made head boy speaks volumes about his leadership abilities. This was borne out by all his adventures and work experiences in his gap year. His confidence enabled him to take on, and cope brilliantly with, life-changing challenges that others wouldn't have even attempted.

What has helped Sam achieve despite the obvious challenges of his dyslexia and his early experience of failure in education? We may say he has grit. This is a buzzword that has become popular in parenting and education circles in the last few years. It has been the focus of the work of neuroscientist and psychologist Angela Duckworth. Duckworth talks about grit as a combination of passion and perseverance. She describes grit as sticking with something for long enough to master it. Duckworth's theory has similarities with Carol Dweck's mindset work. She maintains that grit is more important than talent or IQ and that grit can be learned.

Sam has succeeded, and will no doubt continue to succeed, because he has great self-belief and emotional intelligence.

Sam has courage; in particular, he is not afraid to fail. Without self-belief and willingness to fail children become risk-averse and anxious. Sam is not afraid to fail, not because he has had many experiences of failing, but because he learned that his value is not diminished by his failures. He knows that there is learning in mistakes. He also knows that he is a very capable problem-solver and so is willing to take on challenges like the Mongol Rally because he believes he can handle it.

When I was collecting stories from parents to put in my book *Real Parenting for Real Kids*, I was sent this lovely example.

Eight-year-old Ethan was due to go to an adventure farm for a two-night trip with his school. He had only spent three or four nights away from his mother since birth, and these had all been with family. In addition, Ethan had always been anxious about new situations, finding the first day of term challenging, or being left at parties when he was younger.

Over the last few years, his mother had used emotion coaching and many chat-throughs to help him in new situations. She had also taken every opportunity to encourage self-reliance – and at eight years old he did many tasks for himself.

As the trip approached, she broached the subject of what he might want to take with him, and what he might do there, and how he might feel about being away from her. He told her that he was a little bit worried but mostly, he assured her, he was excited. 'You see, Mummy, I don't need to be too worried, because I am the sort of boy who can do lots of things for himself ...' he said.

Courage is one of the hallmarks of grit. Where does courage come from? Can parents encourage it? Yes, they can.

Elaine and Tony helped Sam cultivate his positive attitude towards failure by refusing to judge him when he got something wrong. Instead they used the Mistakes Process, which is treating what happened as a mistake, helping him to put it right and to learn from it.

Sam was determined to prove the doomsayers wrong. But where does that determination come from? For children to pick themselves up after a failure and try again they have to believe that there is some point in trying. They have to believe that their efforts will pay off. They have to have a growth mindset, some optimism that they can have a positive effect and achieve their goals. If a child does not believe that they can succeed why would they try?

Descriptive praise is a big part of the answer here. When my youngest son first started learning Spanish he had an experience common to many of us. His work came home covered in red ink. This happened so frequently that he formed the belief that he was 'useless' at Spanish and he gave it up at the first opportunity. We need to help our children believe that their efforts make a difference. We need to point out to them where practice has made progress.

Descriptive praise helps kids to see that they can be successful – even if only in small ways. Small successes feed confidence, which leads to greater successes. It is this experience of success that enables them to feel capable. When we focus our praise on efforts, they develop a growth mindset. If we ensure that our praise is non-comparative they will not think they are better than others. When we point out qualities like courage and perseverance, children think of themselves as courageous and determined and act accordingly. One of the things we can help our children with is seeing themselves as successful in overcoming adversity. For example: 'Even though your dam wasn't strong enough the first time, you thought of new ways to make it hold up. You persevered.'

But kids need more than just descriptive praise to develop the self-belief that is such an important part of grit. There are two other important ways parents can encourage grit. To work hard to overcome obstacles one needs to be able to manage one's emotions and one's attention. Self-control is fundamental to the idea of grit and it is encouraged when we build emotional intelligence in our children. We explored this in Chapter 6.

The other thing that parents can do is to encourage self-reliance. Of course, it's much easier, and neater and quicker, if we do things ourselves, but that takes away from our children the opportunity to learn important skills and undermines their confidence. When we let them learn how to do things themselves we tell them we trust you are capable enough for this.

We can do this using multiple micro-skills to help them set up for success. They can be applied to any area of training, whether it be teaching your child to stop sucking their thumb, or to look the teacher in the eye and shake hands, or to remember their sports kit. And as they get older it can be applied to managing their social life and their work schedules. Here are some considerations to take into account when supporting your child's self-reliance:

- We need to have *realistic expectations* of that individual child and what they are capable of at that stage, with their particular temperament and set of challenges, since requiring them to do something that is too far beyond their capabilities is setting up for failure. Of course, it is a judgment call that parents make all the time whether what we're asking is a bit of a stretch (a good thing) or unrealistic.

- *Prepare ahead* of time, rather than just reacting when things go wrong. This means thinking about:

  > *The environment* – are they trying to do homework in too stimulating a setting? Can they reach the hooks to hang up their coat when they get home?

  > *Timing* – when's the best time to pack the school bag for the next day?

  > *How you help them to be independent* – do they need a chart to remind them of their jobs without you nagging? A useful way to think about training children to do things on their own is:

  → I do, you watch (the parent is the pilot).

  → We do (the parent is the co-pilot).

→ You do, I watch (the parent is in the back seat of the cockpit).

→ You do (the parent is no longer in the cockpit).

● *Train in small steps* – get them to practise for ten minutes only to begin with.

● *Practise* – use role plays to prepare for difficult conversations or other tricky situations. My living room was once set up as the interior of a plane to help the Halligans prepare for a long-distance flight.

● *Get your child's input* – it's always better to ask questions to get them thinking than providing all the answers.

● *Use chat-throughs* – this involves asking your child (rather than telling them) what they need to do, in detail, and can be used for anything from homework to a shopping trip or an outing to a theme park or preparing for a new baby. The questions should include what needs to be done and what obstacles may get in the way, including how the child will feel about it. Then brainstorm how to overcome the obstacles.

● Have *family meetings* to celebrate successes and brainstorm problematic areas.

● *Empathise* when they don't want to do something.

● *Descriptively praise* small steps in the right direction.

As Sam, and Ethan, found, when parents train their children to be self-reliant the children get a great gift that says 'I trust you', which allows a child to feel competent and confident. What a thing to have in their rucksacks as they go into the world.

Elaine's reflections

1. For many, success is about academic attainments – good grades, passing exams and getting qualifications – but if our children are to be successful as human beings they

need to be fulfilled and contented. The further education route is not for everyone. Living a successful life is living a happy one. What route can you imagine your child will take in order to find happiness?

2. Letting go is one of the hardest roles parents have to accept. In order to ensure our children are independent and self-reliant, we need to allow them to spread their wings and explore, even though we may feel anxious. Do you struggle to let go? If so, think about the benefits of allowing children to think and act for themselves.

3. Charitable giving has featured a lot in Sam's life since the Mongol Rally, and he has educated himself about important global issues. In what ways can you help your child engage in issues beyond their world?

4. Being brave, taking on challenges and giving things a go is often what parents want/require their children to do. In undertaking the Rickshaw Run, I modelled this behaviour myself, big time! How do you show your child the qualities of persevering and being brave?

5. Sam talks about seeking support and not being embarrassed to reach out for help if you have a hunch something is not right relating to your child. What steps are you going to take as a result of reading this book?

Further reading

Angela Duckworth, *Grit: The Power of Passion and Perseverance*, 2016.

Melissa Hood, *Real Parenting for Real Kids: Enabling Parents to Bring Out the Best in Their Children*, 2016.

Andrew Solomon, *Far from the Tree: Parents, Children and the Search for Identity*, 2013.

Epilogue

Several milestones have been reached since I started writing this book. The summer of 2018 saw Sam graduate from university with a BSc in real estate management. This may not sound like a remarkable achievement to many parents, but we could never have imagined this outcome when we started on this journey. With support from his university, who provided a scribe in the exams, and with access to amazing speech-to-text software, he thrived in an educational environment suited to him and his needs. He studied all aspects of the property sector, from law to planning, and even found himself loving the technical aspects of investment appraisal!

One spring term, he'd attended a presentation given by an estate company. He'd been struck by their philanthropic attitude and their stewardship in looking after a great historic estate in London, so he applied for an internship they were offering. It was highly competitive, and he'd completed his application knowing that the chances of being successful were remote, but considered it good experience all the same.

To everyone's surprise, not least his own, he was called up for interview. He arrived at the office to find seven other candidates there, all from another university. Sam was the only applicant from his university who'd made it this far.

While waiting, the other candidates recounted how they'd attended a presentation here a couple of weeks ago and had been complimented by the director on being dressed for the occasion – suited and booted. The director had then remarked how different this was to when he'd given the same presentation at a university the previous week – the dress code was so casual, one student was even wearing board shorts and flip-flops!

You've guessed it. It had been our Sam. The director had singled him out, judging him on turning up to sit at a presentation in such relaxed attire, unaware that this was the very candidate he'd already chosen to interview.

From two hundred applicants, Sam was awarded one of the two internships. When he received the offer, we danced gleefully around the kitchen table. Then he turned to me, tears brimming in his eyes, and admitted he'd always thought he was unemployable.

Sam is different. But now he owns this difference and he plays to his strengths. He has drive and grit and resilience, gained from all the experiences that shaped him. He suffered brutal failures in his early years, but is now making up for it tenfold, truly living life to the full.

And I am completely different now to the person I was in my twenties. Before I had Sam, I used to judge people for the way they spoke, the car they drove, the clothes they wore and the education they'd had. I admit this with shame, and can only put it down to being hugely impressionable, and determining someone's success in life by their wealth and status.

Over the past couple of decades, I've learned not to judge others, or myself, and not to label too quickly. I have become more confident, able to value my own strengths, and to accept my weaknesses without feeling ashamed or inadequate. Through the positive parenting techniques I learned specifically for Sam, I've ended up developing openness, acceptance and a whole raft of qualities and skills I now use daily with everyone I meet, such as:

- emotional intelligence, so I can now validate other people's feelings instead of being tempted to jump in with advice too quickly;

- a positive attitude, so I can focus on the things I like about a person or something they've done or the way they think, rather than leaping in with criticism;

- a sense of calmness and an ability to cope when things go wrong, when everything around me may be in chaos;

- an ability to problem-solve and always seek new strategies and solutions; and

- a sense of humour! Having always taken myself quite seriously, I have learned to lighten up — and it's about time!

My giving up work as an accountancy lecturer was a huge deal. I came to the realisation that something had to give in order for us to function as a family, but I felt as if I had lost a huge part of my identity. There was a stark dichotomy between my roles as a career woman and a mum. And yet, in an ironic twist, I ended up running a successful business with Melissa, at the forefront of parenting education, which would never have happened had I clung on to accountancy. And I *love* my job!

Wisdom

As I look back on my role as a parent, it's clear I was entirely unprepared for the ride. At times, I felt like my safety belt was loosening, leaving me clinging on for dear life.

I recognise that we did things that at the time that Sam believes may not have been in his best interests. The most significant of these was sending him to the Hawthornes Centre. This was the point at which we had to completely redefine our 'normal'. Having been caught up in the whirlwind of the SEN world, burdened with label upon label and diagnoses, and realising our little boy could not be educated conventionally, this was a key turning point for us. By then, Tony and I had completely lost our confidence as parents. We had no clarity, little knowledge or awareness, and no strategy with which to move forward. Of course, I had significant concerns about some of the techniques adopted at the centre — in particular, the restraining policy — but I had to trust the process. I don't think I'll ever be able to reconcile my feelings about it. There is no doubt that the positive parenting skills we learned there were transformational, but Sam is still dealing with the emotional fallout from his experiences. His contributions to this book brought back many unhappy memories for him. He forgives us, and is a competent, confident and emotionally intelligent young man, so we hope he is able to work through these negative feelings, free to live his life fully.

I also acknowledge now that the non-stop learning support Sam received while at Knowl Hill may have contributed to a learned helplessness, hindering his progress towards becoming an independent learner. Sam is sure that the arrangement was a mistake:

Having a learning support assistant at school wasn't the problem, but there should be a defined line between home and school, otherwise the boundaries become confused. Hayley was with me 24/7 and I sort of latched onto her. It gave me an excuse not to broaden my horizons, cooperate or make any friends.

However, sometimes only hindsight can teach us that we may not have made the best choices.

A pivotal piece in securing the right educational environment for Sam was his statement of SEN. It was a hard-hitting, no-holds-barred presentation of his learning issues and behavioural problems, and without it we wouldn't have been able to access the exceptional support that helped turn Sam's life around. But labels stick. At The Parent Practice, I speak to many parents who are nervous about getting a diagnosis that labels a child, as there's a risk of it becoming a self-fulfilling prophecy: because they have ADHD they are impulsive, and therefore their behaviour needs to be excused. I do believe diagnoses are useful to access the right educational needs at the time, and to facilitate understanding of behavioural traits and how to deal with them, but they must not be used as excuses or to stigmatise.

Sam's statement also prevented him from accessing a good secondary school, reading as if he had unmanageable emotional and behavioural issues. If we had not managed to get it rewritten, who knows what the outcome would have been? The key is to find someone within the LEA you can work with, and start from what *you* need to achieve.

Our experience opened my eyes to the importance of learning the 'soft' skills – life skills – for giving children the positive edge. Despite coming from an academic background myself, I now believe that many schools focus to an unhealthy degree on core academic subjects (sciences, humanities, maths, English) to the exclusion of other valuable learning. For example, creative subjects tend to be considered less important and life skills are commonly ignored. What use is it if your young adult has been tutored, taught and trained to within an inch of his life to get into Oxbridge, only to find on arriving there that they lack the pragmatic skills to actually survive – let alone thrive – in real life? Knowing how to cook for yourself, manage finances, wash a jumper and change a fuse or a car tyre are essential life skills. It's also vital for their success academically as well as personally that they learn to understand other perspectives, think creatively and problem-solve. If they are going to be leaders they need to have good emotional intelligence. We do our children no favours when we educate them narrowly. As Mark Twain put it, 'I never let my schooling get in the way of my education.'

Of course the biggest landmark moment for us was finding a school with inspiring, forward-thinking teachers who tailored their approach to each child. This environment was the key to unlocking Sam's potential.

Holland

At the start of this book, I quoted Emily Perl Kingsley's short essay 'Welcome to Holland'. A decade on, someone has anonymously written a follow-up story and I hope that, together with my story, this final passage provides you with hope and optimism.

Welcome to Holland (Part 2)

I have been in Holland for over a decade now. It has become home. I have had time to catch my breath, to settle and adjust, to accept something different than I'd planned.

I reflect back on those years past when I had first landed in Holland. I remember clearly my shock, my fear, my anger – the pain and uncertainty. In those first few years, I tried to get back to Italy as planned, but Holland was where I was to stay. Today, I can say how far I have come on this unexpected journey. I have learned so much more. But, this too has been a journey of time. I worked hard. I bought new guidebooks. I learned a new language and I slowly found my way around this new land. I have met others whose plans had changed like mine, and who could share my experience. We supported one another and some have become very special friends. Some of these fellow travellers had been in Holland longer than I and were seasoned guides, assisting me along the way. Many have encouraged me. Many have taught me to open my eyes to the wonder and gifts to behold in this new land. I have discovered a community of caring.

Holland wasn't so bad. I think that Holland is used to wayward travellers like me and grew to become a land of hospitality, reaching out to welcome, to assist and to support newcomers like me in this new land. Over the years, I've wondered what life would have been like if I'd landed in Italy as planned. Would life have been easier? Would it have been as rewarding? Would I have learned some of the important lessons I hold today? Sure, this journey has been more challenging and at times I would (and still do) stomp my feet and cry out in frustration and protest. And, yes, Holland is slower paced than Italy and less flashy than Italy, but this too has been an unexpected gift. I have learned to slow down in ways too and look closer at things, with a new appreciation for the remarkable beauty of Holland with its tulips, windmills and Rembrandts. I have come to love Holland and call it Home. I have become a world traveller and discovered that it doesn't matter where you land. What's more important is what you make of your journey and how you see and enjoy the very special, the very lovely, things that Holland, or any land, has to offer. Yes, over a decade ago I landed in a place I hadn't planned. Yet I am thankful, for this destination has been richer than I could have imagined!

Anonymous

Resources

It is my intention that this book brings you hope and optimism. If it has, it may also leave you wanting to explore certain topics more, especially if you are starting to realise for the first time that you have an atypical learner, or a 'different' or 'difficult' child. I know it's easy to become overwhelmed with the amount of information out there and, if you're anything like me, my bedside table still groans with the weight of books about child development and parenting. So, like a trusted friend, I want to give you my top list of resources (many of which have been mentioned throughout this book) that I believe are worth investigating as and when the time feels right for you.

For information on specific learning difficulties:

- Mary Sheedy Kurcinka, *Raising Your Spirited Child: A Guide for Parents Whose Child Is More Intense, Sensitive, Perceptive, Persistent, and Energetic*, 3rd edition, 2016.
- Carol Stock Kranowitz, *The Out-of-Sync Child: Recognizing and Coping with Sensory Processing Disorder*, 2005.

For positive parenting skills and tips for success:

- Angela Duckworth, *Grit: The Power of Passion and Perseverance*, 2016.
- Carol S. Dweck, *Mindset: Changing the Way You Think to Fulfil Your Potential*, updated edition, 2017.
- Bonnie Harris, *When Your Kids Push Your Buttons: And What You Can Do About It*, 2005.
- Melissa Hood, *Real Parenting for Real Kids: Enabling Parents to Bring Out the Best in Their Children*, 2016.

To experience what it feels like to be dyslexic, this website offers a simulation of what a dyslexic child experiences when they try to read (and also provides access to the fabulous Parent Toolkit resource):

- www.understood.org

For free, independent advice on EHC plans and SEN:

- SOS!SEN – the independent helpline for special educational needs – www.sossen.org.uk

- Special Needs Jungle – providing resources, training and information for parents and carers of children and young people with special needs and disabilities – www.specialneedsjungle.com

For information on special needs schools:

- The Good Schools Guide – www.goodschoolsguide. co.uk/special-educational-needs (they also offer a SEN consultancy service)

For information on IT support for dyslexia:

- Achieve Now – www.achievenow.org.uk

For resources on looking after *you* and making yourself an important resource:

- Project Me for Busy Mothers – www.myprojectme.com

For all you adventurists out there (over-18s only!):

- The Adventurists – www.theadventurists.com

And finally, for more information and positive parenting support, for your child who is different:

- Visit www.theparentpractice.com to read The Parent Practice's blogs and latest articles in the press and to watch their recent appearances in the media

- Join The Parent Practice on Facebook to check out the latest ideas and strategies for bringing out the best in your children at www.facebook.com/theparentpractice

- Follow The Parent Practice's musings on Twitter at www.twitter.com/ParentPractice

- Connect with me on LinkedIn at www.linkedin.com/in/elainehalligan

- Bring me in as a guest speaker to your school, conference or corporate event

And finally please join me in celebrating all the unique qualities children who are different can bring to society.

References

Branson, R. (2011). *Screw It, Let's Do It: Lessons in Life*. London: Virgin Books.

Branson, R. (2017). Richard Branson: Dyslexia Is Merely Another Way of Thinking, *The Times* [blog] (30 April). Available at: https://www.thetimes.co.uk/article/richard-branson-dyslexia-is-merely-another-way-of-thinking-8tlmgsndw.

Duckworth, A. (2016). *Grit: The Power of Passion and Perseverance*. London: Vermilion.

Dweck, C. S. (2015). The Secret to Raising Smart Kids, *Scientific American* (1 January). Available at: https://www.scientificamerican.com/article/the-secret-to-raising-smart-kids1/.

Dweck, C. S. (2017). *Mindset: Changing the Way You Think to Fulfil Your Potential*, updated edition. New York: Ballantine.

Faber, A. and Mazlish, E. (2013). *How to Talk so Kids Will Listen and Listen so Kids Will Talk*. London: Piccadilly Press.

Ginott, H. G. (2003). *Between Parent and Child: The Bestselling Classic That Revolutionized Parent–Child Communication* (revised and updated by Dr Alice Ginott and Dr H. Wallace Goddard). New York: Three Rivers Press.

Goleman, D. (2009). *Emotional Intelligence: Why It Can Matter More than IQ*. London: Bloomsbury.

Goleman, D. (2014). *What Makes a Leader: Why Emotional Intelligence Matters*. Florence, MA: More Than Sound.

Gottman, J. M. and DeClaire, J. (1998). *Raising an Emotionally Intelligent Child: The Heart of Parenting*. New York: Simon & Schuster.

Gottman, J. M. and Schwartz Gottman, J. (2008). *And Baby Makes Three: The Six-Step Plan for Preserving Marital Intimacy and Rekindling Romance After Baby Arrives*. New York: Three Rivers Press.

Harris, B. (2005). *When Your Kids Push Your Buttons: And What You Can Do About It*. London: Piatkus.

Hartley-Brewer, E. (2005). *Raising and Praising Boys*. London: Vermilion.

Hood, M. (2016). *Real Parenting for Real Kids: Enabling Parents to Bring Out the Best in Their Children.* Bramley: Practical Inspiration Publishing.

Kohn, A. (1999). *Punished by Rewards: The Trouble with Gold Stars, Incentive Plans, A's, Praise and Other Bribes.* New York: Houghton Mifflin Harcourt.

Markham, L. (2013). *Peaceful Parent, Happy Kids: How to Stop Yelling and Start Connecting.* New York: TarcherPerigee.

Morehead, J. (2012). Stanford University's Carol Dweck on the Growth Mindset and Education, *OneDublin.org* (19 June). Available at: https://onedublin.org/2012/06/19/stanford-universitys-carol-dweck-on-the-growth-mindset-and-education/.

Sheedy Kurcinka, M. (2016). *Raising Your Spirited Child: A Guide for Parents Whose Child Is More Intense, Sensitive, Perceptive, Persistent, and Energetic,* 3rd edition. New York: HarperCollins.

Siegel, D. J. and Bryson, T. P. (2014). *No Drama Discipline: The Whole-Brain Way to Calm the Chaos and Nurture Your Child's Developing Mind.* London: Scribe.

Solomon, A. (2013). *Far from the Tree: Parents, Children and the Search for Identity.* New York: Simon & Schuster.

Stock Kranowitz, C. (2005). *The Out-of-Sync Child: Recognizing and Coping with Sensory Processing Disorder.* New York: Penguin.

About the Author

Elaine Halligan is a director at The Parent Practice and has been a parenting specialist since 2006, helping parents raise competent and confident children through parenting classes, private coaching and keynote speaking in schools and corporate settings both in the UK and overseas. She is frequently quoted in the broadsheet press and regularly appears on Sky News, BBC world news and BBC local radio. Her mission is to help parents find the holy grail of parenting: keeping calm and bringing out the best in their children.

www.theparentpractice.com